YOUR recipe could appear in our next cookbook!

Share your tried & true family favorites with us instantly at

www.gooseberrypatch.com

If you'd rather jot 'em down by hand, just mail this form to...
Gooseberry Patch • Cookbooks – Call for Recipes
PO Box 812 • Columbus, OH 43216-0812

If your recipe is selected for a book, you'll receive a FREE copy!

Please share only your original recipes or those that you have made your own over the years.

Recipe Name:

Number of Servings:

Any fond memories about this recipe? Special touches you like to add or handy shortcuts?

Ingredients (include specific measurements):

Instructions (continue on back if needed):

Special Code: **cookbookspage**

Over ↗

Extra space for recipe if needed:

Tell us about yourself...

Your complete contact information is needed so that we can send you your FREE cookbook, if your recipe is published. Phone numbers and email addresses are kept private and will only be used if we have questions about your recipe.

Name:

Address:

City: State: Zip:

Email:

Daytime Phone:

Thank you! Vickie & Jo Ann

Gooseberry Patch

Fun Fall Foods

A harvest celebration of delicious recipes, plus clever ideas for seasonal fun with family & friends.

Gooseberry Patch

An imprint of Globe Pequot
246 Goose Lane
Guilford, CT 06437

www.gooseberrypatch.com

1•800•854•6673

Copyright 2021, Gooseberry Patch 978-1-62093-425-8

Do you have a tried & true recipe...

tip, craft or memory that you'd like to see featured in
a **Gooseberry Patch** cookbook? Visit our website at
www.gooseberrypatch.com and follow the
easy steps to submit your favorite family recipe.
Or send them to us at:

Gooseberry Patch
PO Box 812
Columbus, OH 43216-0812

Don't forget to include the number of servings your recipe makes,
plus your name, address, phone number and email address. If we
select your recipe, your name will appear right along with it...
and you'll receive a **FREE** copy of the book!

Contents

Dedication

*To everyone who loves county fairs, homecoming
games, leaf peeping, trick-or-treating and Turkey Day...
and all the scrumptious foods that go with them.*

Appreciation

*A hearty thanks for all of you who opened your recipe
boxes and shared your tastiest dishes of the season.*

Chilly Morning
Breakfasts

ABC Pancakes

Ginny Watson
Scranton, PA

On the first day of school, my kids always just loved it when I made these pancakes, marked with their initials! We still have fun making pumpkin face pancakes for Halloween too.

2 c. biscuit baking mix
1 c. milk

2 eggs, beaten
Garnish: butter, pancake syrup

In a bowl, whisk together biscuit mix, milk and eggs until well mixed. Pour about 1/2 cup batter into a plastic squeeze bottle with a narrow tip; set aside. Heat a lightly greased griddle over medium heat. Squeeze batter from squeeze bottle onto hot griddle to form a letter of the alphabet, remembering to make the letter backwards. Cook just until golden on the bottom; pour 1/4 cup batter over the "letter." Cook until bubbles appear at the edges; turn and cook other side until golden. Serve with butter and syrup. Makes 6 servings.

Make school-day breakfasts fun! Cut the centers from a slice of toast with a cookie cutter, serve milk or juice with twisty straws or put a smiley face on a bagel using raisins and cream cheese.

Silver Dollar Pumpkin Pancakes
Jill Valentine
Jackson, TN

*My little boy was so tickled the first time I made
these tiny pancakes...he ate a dozen of them!*

2 eggs
1 c. milk
1/2 c. canned pumpkin
1/4 c. canola oil
1-3/4 c. biscuit baking mix

2 T. sugar
1/2 t. ground ginger
1/2 t. cinnamon
1/2 t. nutmeg
Garnish: butter, pancake syrup

In a bowl, beat eggs with an electric mixer on high speed for 3 to
5 minutes, until thick and lemon-colored. Reduce speed to medium;
beat in milk, pumpkin and oil. Add biscuit mix, sugar and spices; beat
on low speed until well blended. Pour batter by tablespoonfuls onto a
lightly greased griddle over medium heat. For full-size pancakes, pour
batter by 1/4 to 1/2 cupfuls. Cook until puffy and bubbles begin to
form around the edges. Turn and cook other side until golden. Serve
pancakes garnished as desired. Makes about 5 dozen mini pancakes.

Breakfast sliders! Whip up your favorite pancake batter and
make silver dollar-size pancakes. Sandwich them together
with slices of heat & serve sausage. Serve with maple syrup
on the side for dipping...yum!

Sausage Crescent Rolls

Dana Rowan
Spokane, WA

I have a teenage son who is always hungry! When his friends come over, they devour everything in my pantry. I learned that tucking pretty much any filling (even leftover casserole) into a crescent roll is a quick, inexpensive way to feed a lot of people. This recipe is so easy and delicious!

1 lb. mild or spicy ground pork
    breakfast sausage
8-oz. pkg. cream cheese,
    softened

2 8-oz. tubes refrigerated
    crescent rolls
1 egg white, lightly beaten

Lightly brown sausage in a skillet over medium heat; drain. While sausage is still hot, add cream cheese. Stir until cheese is melted and mixture is creamy. Remove from heat; cool completely. Unroll crescent rolls; arrange into 2 rectangles. Form a log of sausage mixture lengthwise down the center of each rectangle. Fold over the long sides to cover each sausage log. Place rolls seam-side down on an ungreased baking sheet. Brush with egg white. Bake at 350 degrees for 20 minutes, or until crust is golden. Allow to cool completely; slice one to 1-1/2 inches thick. Makes 10 to 20 pieces.

Serve up eggs in toasty mini bread bowls! Fun to eat and perfect for a brunch table. Cut the tops off crusty dinner rolls, hollow them out and brush with butter. Fill with a sprinkle of cheese and bacon bits, then break an egg into the roll. Wrap in aluminum foil and pop into a 375-degree oven for 20 minutes, or until egg is set.

Chilly Morning
Breakfasts

Mini Hashbrown Casseroles

Wendy Jacobs
Idaho Falls, ID

*Portioned just right to grab & go in the morning...
perfect for brunch buffets too.*

16-oz. pkg. ground pork
    breakfast sausage, cooked
    and crumbled
1/2 c. green pepper, diced
4 eggs
1/2 c. milk

1/2 t. pepper
20-oz. pkg. refrigerated
    shredded hashbrowns
3 T. butter, melted and slightly
    cooled
1 c. shredded Cheddar cheese

Brown sausage with green pepper in a skillet over medium heat; drain well. Meanwhile, whisk together eggs, milk and pepper in a large bowl. Add sausage mixture and remaining ingredients; mix well. Spoon mixture into lightly greased muffin cups, filling 2/3 full. Bake at 350 degrees for 25 to 30 minutes, until eggs are set and a toothpick inserted in the center tests clean. Makes one to 1-1/2 dozen.

Fall has always been my favorite time of year. In my day there were no school buses...we had to walk to and from school. Some of my fondest memories are those walks home from school. If we were lucky, maybe on a stormy day a parent would drive us. My mom, who loved to bake just about every day, would put the baked goods on a table in our breezeway to cool. Wafting toward me on my walk up the driveway was the sweet aroma of that day's baking. We could hardly wait for dinnertime to dive into those sweet treats!

– Pattie Bryan Harris, Talladega, AL

Pigs in a Straw House

Rudie Shahinian
Ontario, Canada

This old-fashioned breakfast casserole is sure to satisfy a hungry family! It's great for dinner too. The sweet name was inspired by the Three Little Pigs story and makes it fun for kids.

6 eggs
1/2 c. milk
2 c. cooked ham, cubed
2 c. shredded Cheddar cheese
3 T. butter, melted and cooled
   slightly

4 c. French bread, cubed
1 t. dried oregano
1 t. dried thyme
1 t. dried rosemary
1/4 t. allspice
salt and pepper to taste

Whisk together eggs and milk in a large bowl. Add remaining ingredients; mix well. Spoon mixture into a buttered 13"x9" baking pan. Bake, uncovered, at 350 degrees for 30 to 35 minutes, until golden and eggs are set. Makes 8 servings.

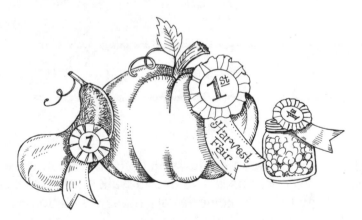

There are so many fun harvest festivals, antique sales and county fairs every autumn...be sure to visit at least one! A hearty breakfast together with family & friends will start the day off right.

Rich Ed's Biscuit & Gravy Scramble

Sheri Kohl
Wentzville, MO

My husband Rich loves his biscuits & gravy and mixes everything together on his plate. I came up with the perfect casserole which includes all his favorite ingredients already mixed together! When I took this dish to a church group brunch, I was overwhelmed with requests by women wanting to make it for their husbands too.

1 lb. ground pork breakfast
    sausage
2-3/4 oz. pkg. country sausage
    gravy mix
16.3-oz. tube refrigerated jumbo
    biscuits, quartered

1 c. shredded Cheddar cheese
6 eggs
1/2 c. milk
salt and pepper to taste

Brown sausage in a skillet over medium heat; drain well. Prepare gravy mix according to package directions; set aside. Spread biscuit quarters in the bottom of a 13"x9" baking pan sprayed with non-stick vegetable spray. Sprinkle with sausage and cheese. Beat together eggs, milk, salt and pepper; pour over ingredients in pan. Pour gravy over all. Bake, uncovered, at 350 degrees for 30 to 45 minutes, until hot and bubbly. Makes 8 servings.

Start a tailgating Saturday right...invite friends to join you for breakfast! Keep it simple with a breakfast casserole, baskets of muffins and a fresh fruit salad on the menu. It's all about food and friends!

Crustless Bacon-Swiss Quiche

Janine Kuras
Warren, MI

I made this delicious quiche for a tailgating brunch...
it was quite a hit with everyone!

9 eggs, beaten
3 c. milk
1 t. dry mustard
salt and pepper to taste
9 slices white bread,
    crusts trimmed

1-1/2 c. Swiss cheese, diced
1 lb. bacon, crisply cooked
    and crumbled
Optional: diced green onion

Combine eggs, milk, mustard, salt and pepper in a large bowl; blend well. Tear bread into small pieces; add to egg mixture along with cheese, bacon and green onion, if using. Spoon into a greased 13"x9" baking pan or 2 greased 9" glass pie plates. Cover and refrigerate 2 hours to overnight. Uncover and bake at 350 degrees for 45 to 50 minutes, until eggs have set. Cut into squares or wedges. Makes 12 servings.

Hang an old-fashioned peg rack inside the back door,
then hang up all the kids' backpacks plus a tote bag for yourself.
Gather schoolbooks, permission slips, car keys and other
important stuff before you go to bed. Less morning rush...
more time to enjoy breakfast!

Chilly Morning

Breakfasts

Baked Eggs with Spinach

Phyl Broich-Wessling
Garner, IA

This is a very good breakfast egg bake...even picky eaters will like it!
Serve with fresh fruit cups or cherry tomatoes, toasted English
muffins and crisp bacon for a great start to your day.

4 green onions, sliced
1/2 green pepper, chopped
2 cloves garlic, minced
10-oz. pkg frozen chopped
    spinach, thawed and drained
1/2 c. half-and-half
salt and pepper to taste

1 doz. eggs
2 c. shredded mozzarella cheese
14-1/2 oz. can crushed tomatoes
1/2 c. hot or mild salsa
1 T. extra-virgin olive oil
1/2 t. cayenne pepper

In a large skillet sprayed with non-stick olive oil spray, combine green onions, green pepper, garlic and spinach. Cook over medium heat, stirring often, until tender. Stir in half-and-half; season with salt and pepper to taste. Spoon mixture into a lightly greased 13"x9" baking pan. With the back of a small spoon, make 12 slight indentations in mixture, spacing evenly. One egg at a time, carefully break eggs into a cup without breaking yolk; pour eggs into the indentations. Sprinkle with cheese. Combine remaining ingredients in a saucepan; season with additional salt and pepper. Warm through over medium-low heat; spoon over cheese layer. Bake, uncovered, at 350 degrees for 10 to 15 minutes, until eggs are set. Makes 6 to 8 servings.

A warm fruit compote is delightful with breakfast. Simmer
sliced peaches, blueberries and raspberries together with
a little honey, lemon juice and cinnamon, just until syrupy
and tender. Divine made with fresh ripe fruit...
scrumptious made with frozen fruit too.

Birthday Baked French Swirl Toast

Gladys Kielar
Whitehouse, OH

We've enjoyed this baked French toast for birthday breakfasts. It's a great choice for any special day and when guests come for an overnight visit.

16-oz. loaf cinnamon swirl
   bread, cubed
3/4 c. sweetened dried
   cranberries
6 eggs, beaten

3 c. half-and-half or milk
2 t. vanilla extract
Garnish: cinnamon-sugar or
   powdered sugar, whipped
   butter, maple syrup

Combine bread cubes and cranberries in a greased shallow 3-quart casserole dish. In a bowl, whisk together eggs, half-and-half or milk and vanilla; pour over bread mixture. Cover and refrigerate for one hour to overnight. Uncover; bake at 350 degrees for 45 minutes, or until golden and set in the center. Sprinkle with cinnamon-sugar or powdered sugar. Serve topped with whipped butter and maple syrup. Makes 8 servings.

Serve your fluffy hotcakes or waffles with flair...instead of setting a plastic bottle on the table, serve warm syrup in small cream pitchers or a vintage syrup server.

Spicy Pumpkin Waffles

Becky Drees
Pittsfield, MA

Welcome the pumpkin season with these tender, delicious waffles!
Splurge with a dollop of whipped cream and a sprinkle of cinnamon.

1-1/3 c. whole-wheat pastry
   flour
2 T. plus 2 t. sugar
2 t. baking soda
1/8 t. salt
2 t. cinnamon
1 t. nutmeg
1 t. ground ginger

4 egg whites, beaten
1 c. canned pumpkin
1 c. low-fat buttermilk
1/2 c. semi-sweet chocolate
   chips
Garnish: maple syrup or vanilla
   yogurt
Optional: toasted pumpkin seeds

In a small bowl, stir together flour, sugar, baking soda, salt and spices; set aside. In a separate bowl, whisk together egg whites, pumpkin and buttermilk; stir in chocolate chips. Add to flour mixture; stir just to combine. Heat a waffle iron until hot; spray with non-stick vegetable spray. Add batter to waffle iron by 1/2 cupfuls; bake according to manufacturer's instructions. Repeat with remaining batter. Serve waffles topped with maple syrup or yogurt; sprinkle with pumpkin seeds, if desired. Makes 4 large waffles or 8 pancakes.

Spice up an autumn breakfast with cider-glazed sausages.
Brown and drain 1/2 pound of breakfast sausage links. Add
a cup of apple cider to the skillet, then turn the heat down
to low and simmer for 10 minutes. Yummy!

Honey Apple Pancakes

Susan Kruspe
Hall, NY

A lovely fall treat! I sometimes share a basket with the recipe, the dry mix, a bottle of apple juice and a can of homemade chunky applesauce. Great for a new neighbor or just "Thinking of you!"

1-1/4 c. all-purpose flour
2 t. baking powder
1/8 t. baking soda
1/4 t. salt
1/4 t. apple pie spice
1 egg, beaten

3/4 c. apple juice
2 T. honey
1 T. oil
Garnish: warmed maple syrup
    or applesauce

In a bowl, combine flour, baking powder, baking soda, salt and spice; set aside. In another bowl, whisk together egg, apple juice, honey and oil. Add egg mixture to flour mixture; mix just until moistened. Pour batter by 1/4 cupfuls onto a lightly greased hot griddle. Cook for 2 to 3 minutes on each side. Serve pancakes with warm maple syrup or warm applesauce. Makes 8 pancakes.

French Toast Pick-Up Sticks

Jen Thomas
Santa Rosa, CA

Our kids love this French toast they can eat with their hands! Save time by making ahead and freezing. Pop in the toaster to serve.

2 eggs, beaten
3/4 c. milk
1 t. vanilla extract
4 slices bread, each cut into
    4 strips

1 T. butter
Garnish: maple syrup, favorite
    preserves

Whisk together eggs, milk and vanilla in a shallow bowl. Dip bread strips, soaking well. Melt butter in a skillet over medium heat. Add bread strips; cook until golden on both sides. Serve warm with syrup or preserves for dipping. Makes 2 to 4 servings.

Chilly Morning
Breakfasts

Blueberry Buckwheat Pancakes

Lynnette Jones
East Flat Rock, NC

Buckwheat pancakes just taste like fall! Feel free to use your own favorite fresh or frozen berries.

1-1/2 c. buckwheat flour
1/2 t. baking powder
1/2 t. baking soda
1/4 t. salt
1 c. buttermilk
2 egg whites, beaten

1 egg, beaten
1 T. honey
1 T. canola oil
1 t. vanilla extract
1 c. blueberries, thawed if frozen
Garnish: maple syrup, fresh fruit

In a bowl, mix flour, baking powder, baking soda and salt. In a separate bowl, stir together buttermilk, egg whites, egg, honey, oil and vanilla. Add buttermilk mixture to flour mixture; stir well. Gently fold in blueberries. Heat a lightly greased skillet over medium heat. Add batter by 1/4 cupfuls. Cook until bubbles appear on top, about 1-1/2 minutes. Turn; cook other side until golden, about 1-1/2 minutes. Top with more fresh fruit or maple syrup, if desired. Serves 4.

For extra-special pancakes or French toast, whip up some maple butter in no time. Just blend 1/2 cup butter with 3/4 cup maple syrup.

Chocolate Gravy & Crescents

Sherry Sheehan
Phoenix, AZ

My brother makes a similar recipe for breakfast every year on the day after Thanksgiving. I never could get him to share his exact recipe, so I made up this recipe based on the taste and a couple secrets that I knew he used. I think it is pretty close. It is a wonderful breakfast for special occasions. The gravy can be served over biscuits, but I enjoy the richness that the crescent rolls give it. We always serve crispy bacon alongside this dish.

8-oz. tube refrigerated crescent rolls	1/4 c. sugar
5 T. butter, sliced	1-1/4 c. milk
3 T. all-purpose flour	1-1/2 t. vanilla extract
3 T. dark baking cocoa	1/4 t. salt

Bake crescent rolls according to package directions; cool. Meanwhile, melt butter in a saucepan over medium heat. Add flour, cocoa and sugar; whisk together until smooth. Add milk to saucepan; continue whisking until smooth. Cook for 2 minutes, or until thickened and smooth. Add a little more milk if gravy becomes thicker than desired. Remove from heat; stir in vanilla and salt. Serve chocolate gravy ladled over warm crescent rolls. Serves 4.

Fall is sweater weather, so keep a cozy sweater on a hook near the back door and enjoy an early-morning walk after breakfast.

Apple Butter Drop Biscuits

Andrea Heyart
Savannah, TX

Every autumn I make a big batch of homemade apple butter and love to find unique ways to use it. These easy drop biscuits are one of my tastiest creations. They're scrumptious served with breakfast, with a barbecue dinner or hot out of the oven anytime!

2 c. all-purpose flour
1 T. sugar
2 t. baking powder
1/2 t. baking soda
3/4 t. salt

1 t. cinnamon
1/2 c. butter, melted
1 c. apple butter
1/3 c. buttermilk

Combine flour, sugar, baking powder, baking soda, salt and cinnamon in a large bowl; mix well and set aside. In a separate bowl, stir together melted butter, apple butter and buttermilk. Stir into flour mixture until batter is thick and sticky. Drop batter onto a greased or parchment paper-lined baking sheet, using 2 tablespoons batter per biscuit. Bake at 375 degrees for 12 to 15 minutes, until lightly golden. Remove from oven; brush with Butter Baste. Serve warm. Makes one dozen.

Butter Baste:

2 T. butter, melted
1 t. sugar

1 t. cinnamon

Combine all ingredients in a small bowl.

Sing a song of seasons!
Something bright in fall!
Flowers in the summer,
Fires in the fall!

–Robert Louis Stevenson

Ten-Grain Pancakes

Ellie Barton
Colville, WA

We love these pancakes. When we camp at our cabin at the lake, we mix up the batter the night before. In the morning, we cook the pancakes in a cast-iron skillet on the cabin's old wood cookstove. We add fruit from our orchard and garden, and top it all with fresh whipped cream from our Jersey cows. Mixing up the batter the night before works great on school mornings too.

2 c. boiling water
1 c. 10-grain cereal
1/2 c. cornmeal
2 T. molasses, or more to taste
2 c. buttermilk
5 eggs, beaten

2 c. whole-wheat flour
1 c. all-purpose flour
2 T. baking powder
1/2 t. baking soda
1 T. salt
1/3 c. melted butter or canola oil

Pour boiling water over cereal and cornmeal in a large bowl; stir until thickened. Add molasses; stir until cooled. Beat in buttermilk and eggs; set aside. In a separate bowl, combine flours, baking powder, baking soda and salt. Stir in cereal mixture and butter or oil until well mixed; don't overmix. Cover and refrigerate if making batter ahead of time. Drop batter by 1/4 to 1/3 cupfuls onto a lightly greased hot griddle. Cook until golden on both sides. Serves 6.

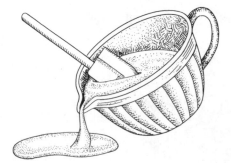

A time-saving tip! Mix up the dry ingredients for your special flapjacks the night before. In the morning, just stir in the milk and eggs while the griddle is heating.

Mulled Cider Syrup

Mardell Lamb
Pavilion, NY

This delicious, spicy pancake & waffle syrup has been a family favorite for many years now. The apple jelly thickens it.

2 c. apple cider
1/4 c. brown sugar, packed
1/4 c. sugar
1/2 c. apple jelly

1/2 t. cinnamon
1/4 t. ground cloves
1/4 t. nutmeg

In a one-quart saucepan over medium heat, combine cider and sugars. Cook over low heat without stirring until sugars dissolve. Stir in apple jelly and spices. Heat to boiling over medium heat. Reduce heat to low; simmer and stir until jelly melts. Remove from heat; cool slightly. Serve warm, or cover and refrigerate until ready to use. Reheat until warm if refrigerated. Makes about 1-1/2 cups.

Cinnamon Syrup

Tina George
El Dorado, AR

This syrup smells so good heating on the stove, we can't wait to put it on our pancakes or French toast! But it's not just for breakfast...try it over apple pie with a scoop of vanilla ice cream.

1/2 c. butter, cubed
1/4 c. maple pancake syrup

3/4 to 1 t. cinnamon

In a small saucepan over low heat, cook butter, syrup and cinnamon until butter is melted. Stir until smooth; serve warm. Makes 4 servings.

The beauty that shimmers in the yellow afternoons of October, who could ever clutch it?

–Ralph Waldo Emerson

Texas Sausage & Green Chile Quiche

Nancy Lozano
Abilene, TX

I found this recipe in one of my favorite cookbooks and added some touches to my taste. Since then, it has been made so many times for brunches, lunches and dinners. We love it!

9-inch deep-dish pie crust,
    unbaked
1/2 lb. ground pork sausage
1/4 c. chopped green onions
4 eggs, beaten
3/4 c. evaporated milk

4-oz. can chopped green chiles
1-1/2 c. shredded Mexican-
    blend cheese
garlic salt, salt and pepper
    to taste

Pierce pie crust with fork; bake at 375 degrees for 5 minutes. Remove from oven; let cool slightly. In a skillet, cook sausage and green onions until sausage is no longer pink; drain. In a large bowl, whisk eggs with evaporated milk. Add chiles, cheese and seasonings; mix well. Spoon into pie crust. Bake at 350 degrees for 40 to 50 minutes, until set. Cut into wedges to serve. Makes 6 servings.

I grew up out in the country with my six siblings in the middle of land that was part of my grandfather's sprawling dairy farm. Those were days of freedom, exploring all over to see what we could discover. One fun fall activity for some of us children was taking old clothes that were ready to be donated to charity, stuffing them with fall leaves, and tying the legs and arms of the clothing with baler twine to form a newfound "friend." Of course, we did all of this after having first made the biggest possible mountain of crispy, crunchy leaves, and diving in several times over!

–Rebecca Reeves, Endicott, NY

Maryland Crab Quiche

*Sandra Monroe
Preston, MD*

This is my husband's favorite recipe. This tasty quiche freezes well, so why not double all the ingredients, make two quiches and freeze one for next week? If freezing, wrap well in aluminum foil and freeze, unbaked. Thaw in the fridge for two hours before baking.

2 eggs, beaten	1/2 lb. crabmeat, flaked
1/2 c. mayonnaise	3/4 c. diced Swiss cheese
2 T. all-purpose flour	1/4 c. shredded Cheddar cheese
1/2 c. milk	1/2 c. sliced green onions
1-1/2 t. seafood seasoning	9-inch pie crust, unbaked

In a bowl, beat together eggs, mayonnaise, flour, milk and seasoning until thoroughly blended. Stir in crabmeat, cheeses and green onions. Spread mixture in unbaked pie crust. Bake at 350 degrees for 40 to 45 minutes, or until a toothpick inserted in center comes clean. Cut into wedges. Makes 6 servings.

Planning a midday brunch? Along with breakfast foods like baked eggs, coffee cake and cereal, offer a light, savory main dish or two for those who have already enjoyed breakfast.

Fun Fall Foods

Cranberry-Pecan Coffee Cake

Georgia Muth
Penn Valley, CA

My sister Diane makes this scrumptious breakfast treat for our family gatherings. Use two cups chopped fresh cranberries, if you have them...no need to cover with hot water.

1 c. sweetened dried cranberries
1 c. boiling water
1-1/2 c. butter, melted
2/3 c. sugar
2 eggs, beaten

1 t. vanilla extract
1-1/2 c. all-purpose flour
1/2 c. toasted pecans
Garnish: powdered sugar

Cover cranberries with hot water; let stand for 10 minutes and drain. In a bowl, combine melted butter and sugar; stir in eggs and vanilla. Add flour and pecans; fold in cranberries. Pour batter into a buttered 8" round springform or torte pan. Bake at 350 degrees for 45 minutes. Cool; dust with powdered sugar. Cut into wedges to serve. Makes 6 to 8 servings.

Breakfast Cookies

Eleanor Dionne
Beverly, MA

These cookies are a little sweet and savory! This is an old recipe that I have started making again. I like the bacon flavor with the other ingredients. It's a great grab & go breakfast.

3-oz. jar bacon bits
1/2 c. butter, softened
1 egg, beaten
2 T. frozen orange juice
   concentrate

1/4 c. sugar
1 c. all-purpose flour
1 t. baking powder
2 c. corn flake cereal
1/4 c. wheat germ

In a large bowl, combine bacon bits, butter, egg, orange juice and sugar. Blend well; stir in remaining ingredients. Shape into one-inch balls. Place on parchment paper-lined baking sheets, about 2 inches apart. Flatten with a fork dipped in flour. Bake at 350 degrees for 12 to 15 minutes, until golden. Makes 2-1/2 dozen.

Mom's Morning Glories

Christine Beauregard
Troy, NH

For years, my mom would make these chockfull-of-goodness muffins for overnight trips and family camping trips. They are satisfying and healthy. Mom doesn't bake anymore, so now I make these muffins for her and Dad when they travel. Don't leave town without 'em!

2-1/2 c. all-purpose flour
1-1/4 c. sugar
1 T. cinnamon
2 t. baking soda
1/2 t. salt
3 eggs, beaten
3/4 c. applesauce
1/2 c. coconut oil or canola oil
1 t. vanilla extract
2 c. carrots, peeled and grated

1 green apple, peeled, cored and grated
8-oz. can crushed pineapple, drained
1/2 c. sweetened dried cranberries, cherries or raisins
1/2 c. sweetened flaked coconut
1/2 c. chopped walnuts

In a large bowl, combine flour, sugar, cinnamon, baking soda and salt; set aside. In a separate bowl, combine eggs, applesauce, oil and vanilla. Add egg mixture to flour mixture; stir well. Fold in remaining ingredients. Spoon batter into greased or paper-lined muffin cups, filling 2/3 full. Bake at 350 degrees for 20 to 24 minutes, until a toothpick in the center tests clean. Cool muffins in muffin tins for 5 minutes; remove muffins to wire racks. Makes 2 dozen.

A baker's secret! Grease muffin cups on the bottoms
and just halfway up the sides...the muffins will
bake up nicely puffed on top.

Sleep-Over French Toast Casserole

Cyndy DeStefano
Mercer, PA

This delicious recipe is great for sleepovers because you prepare it the night before and everyone's breakfast is ready at the same time. Perfect for a group of giggly little girls or hungry boys.

1 loaf French bread, cubed
3-oz. pkg. cream cheese,
   softened
1 c. whipping cream, warmed
1/4 c. maple syrup

6 eggs, beaten
1 t. vanilla extract
1/4 t. cinnamon
1/8 t. salt
Garnish: warmed maple syrup

Place bread cubes in a greased 2-quart casserole dish. Gently press down with a spatula; set aside. In a bowl, beat cream cheese until fluffy. Gradually beat in warm cream and syrup until smooth; set aside. In a separate bowl, whisk together eggs, vanilla, cinnamon and salt; add to cream cheese mixture and blend together. Spoon cream cheese mixture evenly over bread cubes. Use spatula to lightly press bread into cream cheese mixture. Cover and refrigerate for 8 hours to overnight. Remove from refrigerator 15 minutes before baking. Bake, covered, at 375 degrees for 25 minutes. Uncover; bake for another 20 minutes, or until center is set and top is golden. Serve with warmed syrup. Serves 6.

Tickle the kids at breakfast with Jack-o'-Lantern oranges. Slice the tops off navel oranges and scoop out the pulp with a spoon. Draw on silly or spooky faces with food coloring markers. Spoon in fruit salad and serve...clever!

Breakfast Apple Pie

Lori Haines
Johnson City, TN

This pie is actually easier to handle and serve after baking and cooling completely. I like to make it the day before, refrigerate it and warm it up in the microwave to serve. Be sure to serve it warm!

2/3 c. brown sugar, packed
2 T. cornstarch
1 t. cinnamon
1/2 t. nutmeg
1/4 t. ground cloves
2 lbs. Granny Smith apples,
   peeled, cored and diced

9-inch pie crust, unbaked
1/2 lb. bacon, cut into 1-inch
   pieces
1 c. shredded Cheddar cheese

In a large bowl, mix together brown sugar, cornstarch and spices. Add apples; toss to coat well. Spoon into unbaked pie crust. Separate uncooked bacon pieces and layer over apples. Cover loosely with aluminum foil. Bake at 350 degrees for one hour. Remove foil; continue baking for 15 minutes. If bacon is still not crisp enough, place pie under broiler, watching carefully. Allow pie to cool; rewarm before serving. Sprinkle cheese on top of warm pie. Cut into wedges. Makes 6 to 8 servings.

Autumn is time for apple fun. Pick your own apples in an orchard, watch cider being pressed at a cider mill or go to a small-town apple butter stirring. Ask about different varieties of apples... you're sure to find a new favorite!

Breakfast Burritos

Lynda Bolton
East Peoria, IL

My husband came up with this recipe when our preteen kids wouldn't eat the typical bacon, eggs and hashbrowns for breakfast. They loved wraps and Mexican food, so he thought, what if I hide the breakfast ingredients inside a wrap? It became an instant favorite! Nearly 20 years later, the kids still request these whenever they all come back home!

20-oz. pkg. frozen potato puffs
1 lb. sage-flavored ground pork
   sausage
1 doz. eggs
1/3 c. milk
salt and pepper to taste

16-oz. jar salsa
8-oz. pkg. Mexican-style
   pasteurized process cheese,
   cubed
10 to 12 burrito-size flour
   tortillas

Bake potato puffs according to package directions. Meanwhile, in a large skillet, brown sausage over medium-high heat; drain on paper towels. Coarsely chop potato puffs and sausage; set aside. Drain most of drippings from skillet; heat skillet over low heat. In a large bowl, whisk together eggs, milk, salt and pepper until mixed. Pour egg mixture into skillet. Add potato puffs, sausage, salsa and cheese. Cook, stirring occasionally, until eggs are scrambled and cheese is melted. Remove from heat. Microwave tortillas until softened. For each burrito, place one tortilla on a large plate; spoon some of egg mixture into the center. Fold over one edge of tortilla and roll up tightly. Place finished burritos on a platter and serve. Burritos may also be wrapped in plastic wrap and refrigerated or frozen; thaw and microwave until hot. Makes 10 to 12 servings.

Eating breakfast on the run?
Any egg dish turns into a
portable breakfast when rolled
up in a flour tortilla or spooned
into a pita half.

Mexicali Breakfast Potatoes

Vickie
Gooseberry Patch

This hearty potato dish is a wonderful change from ordinary hashbrowns! It's become a tailgating brunch favorite for our family & friends. Garnish with sour cream and a sprinkle of cheese.

32-oz. pkg. frozen diced
   potatoes
1/4 c. onion, diced
1/4 c. red pepper, diced
1/4 c. canned diced green chiles
1 T. Dijon mustard

1-1/4 t. ground cumin
1-1/4 t. salt
1 t. pepper
1/2 t. cayenne pepper
1 T. canola oil

In a large bowl, combine all ingredients except oil; mix well and set aside. Add oil to a large skillet; heat over medium heat. Add potato mixture to skillet. Cook, stirring often, for 12 to 15 minutes, until potatoes are golden. Makes 8 servings.

I love everything about autumn, especially remembering fall traditions. My sister Jan and her family live out in the country. On Halloween, my family would drive to her house with a car full of happy kids, excited for trick-or-treating. We'd get our costumes on and faces painted, then pile outside for picture taking and a walk though her little town. The last stop was always the fire station which was set up as a haunted house with tricks and treats. After the scary fun, there would be hot dogs, cider and doughnuts with the firemen and neighbors. Now every autumn, when pumpkins appear on porches and the air is filled with the smell of wood smoke and apples, leaves crunching underfoot, I am reminded of those special days when little cousins and grown-up sisters had so much fun.

–Pamela Collier, Toledo, OH

Flatbread Breakfast Pizza

Beth Kramer
Port Saint Lucie, FL

My teenagers love to whip up these little breakfast pizzas.
Sometimes we'll add leftover crispy bacon too...yum!

1 egg, beaten
1 T. milk
1 brown & serve breakfast
    sausage link or patty,
    browned and chopped

6-inch round flatbread
2 T. finely shredded Cheddar
    cheese

In a greased 2-cup microwave-safe bowl, whisk together egg and milk; stir in sausage. Microwave on high for 30 seconds; use a spoon to push cooked edges toward center. Microwave for 15 to 45 seconds, until egg is almost set. Turn out egg and slice into 4 to 5 pieces; arrange on flatbread. Sprinkle with cheese. Microwave an additional 10 to 15 seconds, until cheese melts. Makes one serving.

Doughnut hole kabobs...what a delicious idea! Slide bite-size doughnut holes onto wooden skewers and stand the skewers in a tall vase for easy serving.

Chilly Morning

Breakfasts

Mom's Surprise Muffins

Aubrey Nygren
Farmington, NM

*My mom made these muffins for us all the time and we couldn't wait
to find out what filling was waiting inside! We've made them with
peanut butter, fruit jam and even chocolate hazelnut spread. Now
I make them for my own family...they bring back great memories.*

1 egg, beaten
1/2 c. milk
1/4 c. oil
1-1/2 c. all-purpose flour

1/2 c. sugar
2 t. baking powder
1/2 t. salt
1/4 c. peanut butter or jam

In a bowl, whisk together egg, milk and oil; set aside. In a separate
bowl, combine flour, sugar, baking powder and salt. Add flour mixture
to egg mixture; stir just until moistened. Batter will be lumpy. Spoon
batter into 12 greased or paper-lined muffin cups, filling 1/2 full. Drop
one teaspoon peanut butter or jam into the center of each muffin; add
remaining batter to fill cups 2/3 full. Bake at 400 degrees for 20 to
25 minutes, until golden. Immediately remove muffins from pan;
cool slightly. Makes one dozen.

Roly-Polys

Susan Brown
Holly, MI

*This is the first recipe I learned to make in cooking class when
I was in junior high school. Easy to make and yummy too!*

7-1/2 oz. tube refrigerated
  biscuits
2 to 3 T. butter, softened
1 t. cinnamon

1/4 to 1/3 c. sugar
Optional: additional butter,
  melted

Flatten biscuits on a piece of wax paper; spread with butter. In a small
bowl, combine cinnamon and sugar; sprinkle over biscuits. Roll up
biscuits and place on a greased baking sheet. Brush with melted butter,
if desired. Bake at 425 degrees for 10 to 12 minutes, until golden.
Makes 8 servings.

Pumpkin Pie Smoothie

Lisa Ann Panzino DiNunzio
Vineland, NJ

*This smoothie can be put into a covered mug for breakfast
on the go, or serve in a tall glass topped with whipped cream
for the perfect drinkable dessert!*

3/4 c. milk or unsweetened
   almond milk
1/2 c. plain Greek yogurt
2 to 3 T. maple syrup or honey
1/2 c. canned pumpkin

1/2 t. vanilla extract
1/2 t. cinnamon
Optional: 1/8 t. nutmeg
1 c. ice cubes

Combine all ingredients in a blender; process until smooth. Makes
2 servings.

Banana Pudding Smoothie

Courtney Stultz
Weir, KS

*Smoothies are great for quick nutrition, especially for busy families!
This one is wonderful because it tastes like a milkshake...
only healthier! Our whole family loves it.*

1 banana, cut into chunks
8-oz. container plain or vanilla
   yogurt
3/4 c. coconut milk or almond
   milk

1/4 c. chopped almonds
1/2 t. cinnamon
1/8 t. vanilla extract
1/2 c. ice, if desired

Combine all ingredients in a blender. Process for about 30 to
45 seconds, until completely smooth. Makes one serving.

Save bananas that are getting too ripe.
Peel, cut into chunks, wrap in plastic wrap
and tuck in the freezer. Later they can be
tossed into smoothies...no thawing needed.

Indian Summer

Soups & Sandwiches

End-of-the-Garden Soup

Sandra Sullivan
Aurora, CO

So delicious on a cold day! Tuck this soup in your freezer...
a great way to capture fresh summer flavors. Add other
favorite vegetables, if you like.

16 c. tomatoes, diced
2 c. green beans, sliced
2 c. yellow beans, sliced
2 c. carrots, peeled and sliced
1 head cabbage, chopped
1/2 bunch celery, chopped
1 green pepper, chopped
1 onion, chopped
3 c. beef or vegetable broth
3 c. tomato juice
salt and pepper to taste

Combine all ingredients in a large soup pot. Bring to a boil over medium heat; reduce heat to low. Cover and simmer for one hour, stirring occasionally. Season with additional salt and pepper, as desired. Ladle soup into one-quart containers; attach serving directions and freeze. Makes 8 quarts, 4 servings per quart.

To serve: For each thawed one-quart container of soup, brown 1/2 pound ground beef or Italian ground pork sausage; drain. Add soup; bring to a boil. Simmer over low heat for 15 to 20 minutes. Season with additional salt and pepper, as needed.

As a child, I loved going to my grandparents' home, especially in the fall. They had several apple trees and almost always had a bumper crop of apples. My favorite memories are of making homemade apple butter in a big copper kettle over an open flame. We each got to take turns stirring the mixture with a giant wooden paddle. There was nothing better than the smells of fall in the air mingling with the wonderful cinnamon and apple aroma! The process took all day, but we were always up for the task. The best part of the day, however, was getting to taste the fresh apple butter on homemade bread.

–Jennifer Jones, Rochester, IL

Bacon, Potato & Leek Soup

Kathleen Whitsett
Greenwood, IN

When the weather starts to get cold, I like to serve this soup in bread bowls. It's like putting on your favorite fuzzy sweater!

3 leeks, white part only,
   thinly sliced and separated
   into rings
6 slices bacon, diced
2 T. butter, sliced

2 to 3 Yukon Gold potatoes,
   cubed
4 c. chicken broth
1 clove garlic, minced
salt and pepper to taste

In a bowl, cover leeks with cold water to remove any sand; set aside. In a skillet over medium heat, cook bacon until golden but not crisp. With a slotted spoon, remove bacon to a paper towel. Drain skillet, reserving 1-1/2 teaspoons drippings in skillet. Drain leeks; add to skillet along with butter and potatoes. Cook until leeks begin to wilt and potatoes start to soften. Add remaining ingredients. Reduce heat to low. Cover; simmer at least one hour, stirring occasionally, until potatoes are tender. With a potato masher, mash some of the potatoes to thicken soup. Add cooked bacon; season with additional salt and pepper, as needed. Simmer another 15 minutes. Makes 4 servings.

On warm fall days, set up harvest tables and chairs outdoors for a soup supper. Decorate with plump pumpkins, bittersweet wreaths, straw bales and scarecrows. And before the sun sets, end the day with a hayride in the country.

Three Sisters Harvest Stew

Sue Hecht
Roselle Park, NJ

*I have been making this satisfying soup for many years...it's a
favorite of ours. The name comes from the Native American reference
to corn, beans and squash, the three sisters of the Earth. Choose your
favorite beans...black beans are especially good with butternut
squash, while chickpeas go well with yellow squash.*

2 T. olive oil
1 onion, chopped
3 to 4 cloves garlic, chopped
1 carrot, peeled and cut into
   1-inch pieces
3/4 c. butternut squash, cubed,
   or 1 c. yellow or crookneck
   squash, cubed
16-oz. can favorite beans,
   drained

1 c. fresh or frozen corn
1 t. dried sage
sea salt to taste
Optional: 1 dried chipotle
   pepper, or 1/2 t. dried
   chipotle seasoning
2 to 3 c. vegetable broth or
   water, divided
1/4 c. fresh parsley, chopped

Heat oil in a large stew pot over medium heat. Add onion and stir to
coat with oil; sauté until golden. Add remaining vegetables, seasonings
and desired amount of broth or water. Simmer until squash is tender,
adding more broth or water as needed. Add parsley and stir well. Serve
piping hot. Makes 4 to 6 servings.

Just for fun, use a pumpkin as a soup tureen. An all-white
Lumina pumpkin or a plump green and orange Cinderella
pumpkin make the prettiest presentation!

Creamy White Chicken Chili

Katie Black
Freelandville, IN

I lightened up the original recipe by using half-and-half instead of heavy whipping cream and light sour cream to save a little bit of fat. I serve this with a crunchy bread...it's delicious!

1 T. olive oil
1 lb. boneless, skinless chicken
    breast, coarsely shredded
1/2 to 1 c. red onion, chopped
2 cloves garlic, pressed
14-1/2 oz. can chicken broth
2 15-1/2 oz. cans Great
    Northern beans, drained
2 4-oz. cans chopped green
    chiles

1 t. ground cumin
1 t. dried oregano
1 t. salt
1/2 t. red pepper flakes
1/2 t. mixed or black pepper
1/2 c. half-and-half
1 c. light sour cream
Garnish: shredded Monterey
    Jack cheese

Heat oil in a large saucepan over medium heat; add chicken, onion, and garlic. Cook and stir until chicken is no longer pink in the center and juices run clear, 10 to 15 minutes. Add remaining ingredients except half-and-half and sour cream; bring to a boil. Reduce heat to low. Cover and simmer until flavors have blended, stirring occasionally, about 30 minutes. Remove from heat. Stir in half-and-half; fold in sour cream. Garnish individual servings with cheese. Makes 6 servings.

Have some fun with chili toppers. Set out a selection for guests to choose from...diced avocado, sliced jalapeño peppers, shredded Mexican-style cheese and cool sour cream. Don't forget the crushed tortilla chips for crunch!

Italian Bean & Kale Soup

Sue Coppersmith
Granbury, TX

This soup is filling and full of flavor. It can easily be made low-carb by substituting zucchini or yellow squash for the potatoes and cannellini beans.

1 lb. mild Italian pork sausage
    link, casing removed
1/2 c. onion, chopped
4 to 5 cloves garlic, minced
32-oz. container chicken broth
1/2 c. dry white wine or broth
1 to 2 c. Yukon Gold or redskin
    potatoes, cubed

1 to 2 16-oz. cans cannellini
    beans, drained and rinsed
4-1/2 oz. pkg. fresh baby kale
    or spinach
1 t. rosemary, fresh or dried
Garnish: shredded Parmesan
    cheese

Crumble sausage into a stockpot over medium heat; brown and drain. Add onion and garlic. Cook for about one minute, being careful not to burn. Add broth, wine or broth, potatoes and beans. Bring to a simmer. Cover and cook until potatoes are tender, about 15 minutes. Stir in kale or spinach and rosemary. Cook until kale wilts, about 5 minutes. Ladle into bowls; sprinkle each serving with Parmesan cheese. Makes 6 to 8 servings.

Speedy Garlic Cheese Rolls

Sue Klapper
Muskego, WI

These dinner rolls are so fast and easy to make, it's almost embarrassing. In 20 minutes you will have delicious hot rolls!

11-oz. tube refrigerated bread
    sticks
2 T. olive oil

garlic salt to taste
1/2 c. shredded Cheddar cheese
1 egg, beaten

Unroll bread sticks into a rectangle; do not separate. Lightly brush oil over dough; sprinkle with garlic salt and cheese. Gently separate bread sticks. One at a time, roll up bread sticks, pinwheel style; place in a greased muffin cups. Brush tops with beaten egg. Bake at 350 degrees for 15 to 18 minutes, until golden. Makes 8 rolls.

Zucchini Garden Chowder

Judith Jennings
Ironwood, MI

A fun and appealing way to use zucchini. Even picky eaters like it!

2 to 3 zucchini, chopped
1 onion, chopped
1/3 c. butter, cubed
1 T. Italian seasoning, or to taste
1/4 t. pepper
1/3 c. all-purpose flour
3 c. water
1 t. garlic, minced, or to taste
5 cubes chicken bouillon

1 t. lemon juice
14-1/2 oz. can diced tomatoes
12-oz. can evaporated milk
10-oz. pkg. frozen corn
Optional: 1/8 t. sugar
8-oz. pkg. shredded Cheddar
  cheese
Garnish: chopped fresh parsley

In a Dutch oven over medium heat, sauté zucchini and onion in butter until tender. Sprinkle with seasonings. Stir in flour; gradually stir in water, garlic, bouillon and lemon juice. Bring to a boil. Cook and stir for 2 minutes, or until thickened. Add tomatoes with juice, evaporated milk and corn. Bring to a boil. Reduce heat to low. Cover and simmer for 5 minutes, or until corn is tender. Just before serving, stir in sugar, if using. Add cheese; stir until melted. Garnish with parsley. Makes 8 to 10 servings.

Save seeds from this year's garden to plant next spring...it's simple. Collect flowers and seed pods, then shake out the seeds onto paper towels. When they're dry, place seeds in small paper envelopes and seal in canning jars. Don't forget to label them!

Famous Cheeseburger Soup

Hollie Moots
Marysville, OH

There is nothing better on a cool fall day than a big bowl of this soup! It is one of my most-requested recipes. I've been making this soup since my husband and I were first married. It's his absolute favorite and everyone who tries it loves it! Comfort food at its best!

1 lb. ground beef
6 T. butter, sliced and divided
1 c. carrots, peeled and chopped
3/4 c. celery, chopped
1/2 c. onion, chopped
1 t. dried parsley
1 t. dried basil
32-oz. container chicken broth
4 c. potatoes, peeled and diced
1/4 c. all-purpose flour
1-1/2 c. milk
1 t. salt
1/2 t. pepper
9 slices American cheese, chopped
1/4 c. sour cream

Brown beef in a large stockpot over medium heat; drain and set aside. In the same pot, melt 2 tablespoons butter; add carrots, celery, onion and herbs. Sauté until vegetables are tender, about 10 minutes. Return beef to pot; add broth and potatoes. Bring to a boil; reduce heat to medium-low. Cover and simmer for 12 to 15 minutes, until potatoes are tender. Meanwhile, melt remaining butter in a small saucepan over medium heat. Add flour; cook and stir for 2 to 3 minutes. Add butter mixture to soup; return to a boil. Cook and stir for 2 minutes, or until soup is thickened. Reduce heat to medium-low. Stir in milk, salt, pepper and cheese. Cook, stirring occasionally, until cheese is melted. Remove from heat; stir in sour cream. Makes 6 to 8 servings.

Hosting a backyard gathering? Fill a child's little red wagon with ice and tuck in bottles of soda. Use colorful ribbon to tie a bottle opener to the handle so it stays near the drinks.

Tasty Buffalo Chicken Wing Soup

Marcia Donner
East Aurora, NY

This soup warms my family and always reminds us of where we are from...the great city of Buffalo, New York, where the first chicken wing was born! Garnish with chopped celery leaves.

2 to 3 boneless, skinless chicken breasts
2 to 3 potatoes, peeled and diced
2 to 3 carrots, peeled and diced
2 to 3 stalks celery, diced
1/2 c. butter
1/2 c. all-purpose flour

14-oz. can chicken broth
16-oz. container heavy cream
1/4 c. buffalo wing sauce, or to taste
salt and pepper to taste
saltine crackers or sliced bread

Cover chicken with water in a saucepan over medium heat. Cook for 10 to 15 minutes, until juices run clear. Drain and cool; dice chicken and set aside. Meanwhile, in a large soup pot, combine potatoes, carrots and celery. Ad enough water to cover; cook over medium heat until tender. Strain cooking liquid and return to soup pot. Place potato mixture in a food processor; process until smooth. Return potato mixture to reserved liquid in soup pot. Melt butter in a small saucepan over medium heat. Add flour; cook and stir for 2 to 3 minutes. Add butter mixture and broth to soup pot; stir until smooth. Stir in cream, wing sauce and diced chicken. Simmer over low heat for about one hour, stirring occasionally. Season with salt and pepper. Serve with crackers or warm bread for dipping. Makes 6 servings.

Take time to enjoy the simple pleasures of your hometown with family & friends...cookouts, fireworks, festivals and parades!

Unchilly Chili

Melissa Mishler
Columbia City, IN

This chili keeps you warm from the inside-out! I like to serve it on Halloween while sitting on our front porch handing out candy to all the trick-or-treaters.

2 lbs. ground beef
1 onion, finely chopped
1 clove garlic, minced
29-oz. can tomato sauce
28-oz. can diced fire-roasted
  tomatoes
2 cubes beef bouillon
2 1-1/4 oz. pkgs. chili
  seasoning mix

7-oz. can diced green chiles
16-oz. can pinto beans, drained
  and rinsed
Garnish: shredded Cheddar
  cheese, sour cream, minced
  onion, coarsely crushed
  ranch flavor tortilla chips

Brown beef, onion and garlic in a large skillet over medium heat; drain. Add remaining ingredients except garnish; stir well. Cover and cook over low heat for at least one hour, stirring occasionally. Garnish individual servings as desired.. Makes 10 to 12 servings.

On a crisp autumn afternoon, load up a thermos with chili and toss in some lunch-size bags of corn chips, shredded Cheddar cheese and spoons. Take a hike in the woods, then enjoy a portable picnic of chili ladled over the chips and eaten right from the bags. Kids will love it!

Navy Bean Soup

Lori Rosenberg
University Heights, OH

In our house we love to try different soups, but as much as we enjoy something new, this soup is always on the request list. A staple for our family.

1 lb. dried navy beans	2 onions, chopped
8 c. chicken broth	4 carrots, peeled and chopped
2 T. fresh parsley, minced	4 stalks celery, chopped
2 bay leaves	6 slices turkey bacon, crisply
1/4 t. pepper	cooked and crumbled

Place beans in a Dutch oven or soup kettle; add water to cover by 2 inches. Bring to a boil; boil for 2 minutes. Remove from heat; cover and let stand for one hour. Drain and rinse beans; discard liquid. In a large saucepan over medium heat, combine beans, broth, parsley, bay leaves and pepper. Bring to a boil. Reduce heat to low; cover and simmer for one hour, stirring occasionally. Add onions, carrots and celery. Cover and simmer for 20 to 25 minutes, until beans and vegetables are tender. Cool slightly; discard bay leaves. With an immersion-type blender, process soup to desired consistency. Stir in crumbled bacon. Makes 8 to 10 servings.

Dress up a party table with "pumpkins" made of bright orange mums. Trim the stems of real or silk mums to one inch and insert the stems into a large styrofoam ball until it's completely covered. Add a cluster of green leaves at the top for the pumpkin "stem." So eye catching!

Turkey Dumpling Soup

Margo Niccum
Columbus, OH

A delicious day-after-Thanksgiving recipe.

4 c. cooked turkey, chopped
1 onion, chopped
1 green pepper, chopped
1/2 c. celery, chopped
3 c. chicken broth
salt and pepper to taste
3 c. all-purpose flour
2 t. baking powder
1/2 c. oil
1/2 c. water

In a soup pot over medium heat, combine turkey, vegetables and broth. Bring to a boil; simmer until vegetables are tender. Season with salt and pepper. Stir together remaining ingredients in a bowl. Add dough by large spoonfuls to simmering soup. Cook for 8 minutes, or until dumplings are firm. Makes 6 servings.

Comfort Chicken Noodle Soup

Tina Quinnelly
Cowpens, SC

This simple recipe is a favorite of my family. Sure to warm you on chilly autumn evenings!

8 c. water
8 cubes chicken bouillon
12-oz. pkg. egg noodles,
    uncooked and divided
10-3/4 oz. can cream of
    chicken soup
3 c. cooked chicken, cubed
8-oz. container sour cream

In a soup pot over medium-high heat, combine water and bouillon cubes; bring to a boil. Add half of noodles; reserve remaining noodles for another recipe. Cook for 10 minutes, or until noodles are tender. Do not drain. Stir in soup and chicken; heat through. Remove from heat; stir in sour cream. Makes 8 servings.

October's the month when the smallest breeze
Gives us a shower of autumn leaves.

–Unknown

Creamy Chicken & Gnocchi Soup

Katherine Nelson
Centerville, UT

I came up with this recipe after enjoying a similar soup at a local restaurant. My husband had a taste of mine and thought it was good. I loved it and asked for a second bowl! My version is thicker, which my husband likes better. Gnocchi is an Italian dumpling made from mashed potatoes...you'll find them in the Italian section of the grocery store. I hope you like this as much as we do!

1/2 onion, diced
1 stalk celery, diced
1/2 carrot, peeled and shredded
1 clove garlic, diced
1 T. olive oil
3 boneless, skinless chicken breasts, cooked and diced
4 c. chicken broth
2 c. half-and-half

1 T. dried thyme
1/8 t. salt
1/8 t. pepper
16-oz. pkg. gnocchi pasta, uncooked
1/2 c. fresh spinach, chopped
1 T. cornstarch
2 T. cold water

In a large soup pot over medium heat, sauté onion, celery, carrot and garlic in oil until onion is translucent. Stir in chicken, chicken broth, half-and-half and seasonings; bring to a boil. Add gnocchi; cook for 4 minutes. Reduce heat to medium-low. Continue cooking for 10 minutes, stirring often. Add spinach; cook for one to 2 minutes, until spinach is wilted. In a cup, dissolve cornstarch in cold water. Return soup to boiling; add cornstarch mixture. Cook and stir until thickened. Serves 4.

Use caramel apples as festive placecards...rubber stamp a mailing tag, then tie onto the apple's stick with ribbon or raffia.

Cold-Chaser Chicken Soup
Elisabeth Morrissey
Denver, CO

My friends call me to ask for this recipe whenever they get sick. We've found it clears stuffy noses, opens congested chests, settles the stomach and warms you all over. Pure comfort!

2 boneless, skinless chicken
    breasts
8 c. chicken broth
1 c. onion, diced
2 stalks celery, diced
2 carrots, peeled and diced
6 cloves garlic, minced

1/2 to 1-inch piece fresh ginger,
    peeled and minced
1 T. poultry seasoning
1 t. red pepper flakes
salt and pepper to taste
1 c. favorite tri-colored vegetable
    pasta, uncooked

Spray a skillet with non-stick vegetable spray. Add chicken; sauté until no longer pink. Set chicken aside to cool; dice. Meanwhile, in a soup pot over medium-high heat, bring broth to a boil. Stir in vegetables, garlic, ginger and seasonings; reduce heat to low. Cover and simmer for 30 minutes, stirring occasionally. Add diced chicken; cover and simmer for another 30 minutes. Return to a boil; stir in uncooked pasta. Cook over medium-high heat, just until pasta is tender. Makes 8 servings.

Toting some homemade chicken soup to a friend who's under the weather? Remember all the nice things that go along with making someone feel better...crossword puzzles, a book by a favorite author, a box of tissues and a hot water bottle.

Spicy Mexican Chicken Soup

Judy Wilson
Huntsville, AL

This soup uses basic ingredients that are slow-cooked to perfection. We like to serve it with Mexican-blend cheese sprinkled on top and tortilla chips. Feel free to add your own favorite toppings!

3 boneless, skinless chicken
   breasts
2 14-1/2 oz. cans petite diced
   tomatoes
4-oz. can chopped green chiles
2 c. frozen corn
14-1/2 oz. can reduced-sodium
   chicken broth

2 T. chili powder
1 T. ground cumin
1/2 t. salt
1/4 t. cayenne pepper, or to taste
15-oz. can black beans, drained
   and rinsed
Garnish: shredded Mexican-
   blend cheese, tortilla chips

Place chicken in a 4 to 6-quart slow cooker. Add tomatoes with juice, chiles and corn. Pour in broth; add seasonings and stir gently. Cover and cook on low setting for 6 to 7 hours, until chicken is very tender. Remove chicken to a plate; cool and shred. Return shredded chicken to slow cooker and stir well. Add beans; cover and cook on low setting for another 30 minutes. Top with shredded cheese; serve with tortilla chips. Makes 6 servings.

Back-to-school time isn't just for kids. Treat yourself to
a class that you've been longing to try...whether it's
knitting, cooking, yoga or even a foreign language.
Take a girlfriend along for twice the fun!

Bunkhouse Stew

Carolyn Deckard
Bedford, IN

A good friend from work made this slow-cooker soup for supper one night. The next day, she brought me a bowl for lunch, then gave me the recipe. It's so tasty and easy to make.

2 lbs. ground beef
1 onion, diced
3 10-3/4 oz. cans minestrone
   soup
2 14-1/2 oz. cans diced
   tomatoes

15-1/2 oz. can hot chili beans
2-1/2 c. water
Garnish: favorite shredded
   cheese, corn chips

In a skillet over medium heat, brown beef with onion; drain well. Transfer beef mixture to a 6-quart slow cooker. Add soup, undrained tomatoes and undrained beans. Stir in water. Cover and cook on low setting for 5 to 6 hours, until hot and bubbly. Garnish each bowl with shredded cheese or serve with corn chips. Makes 6 to 8 servings.

I was a child in the late 40s and 50s who had an October 30th birthday and a mother who was a leaf peeper. So each year in late October, my parents, younger brother Gary and I drove from Long Island, New York to Kent Falls, Connecticut. Mom got to enjoy the autumn leaves and I got my birthday picnic in Connecticut. We always had our lunch in the park, where Gary and I would play near the stream and on the bridge. We would stop at a nearby cider mill, where the owner would give my brother and me sample glasses of cider while we watched him make it. We always brought home apples, cider, a pumpkin or two and Indian corn for the front door. Then it was really fall and my birthday. I still enjoy looking back at those old black & white photos and reliving those memories.

–Arden Regnier, East Moriches, NY

Bean & Bacon Soup
with a Twist

Koneta Bailey
Hillsboro, OH

This is an extra hearty soup that can be enjoyed all year 'round, and is one of my family's favorite comfort foods. It's budget-friendly and tastes just as good warmed up again...maybe better! I serve it with hot buttered cornbread muffins. Some brands of canned bean & bacon soup may taste saltier than others, so be sure to taste before you add any salt.

1-1/2 lbs. ground beef
1 onion, diced
4 to 5 10-3/4 oz. cans bean &
    bacon soup

4 to 5 c. water
Optional: salt to taste

In a Dutch oven over medium heat, brown beef and onion; drain. Stir in soup and water. Cook over medium heat, stirring often, until heated through and soup has reached the desired consistency. Season with salt, if desired. Makes 8 to 10 servings.

October is the ideal time to plant daffodils, tulips and other spring flowering bulbs! There are lots of varieties to choose from at the neighborhood garden center. Make it a family project... afterwards, warm up with mugs of hot soup.

Cauliflower Thyme Soup

Mindy Powell
Saratoga Springs, UT

We make this soup every Halloween for our family! We enjoy it
with cheesy toasted baguettes to dip in the soup.

4 T. butter, sliced and divided
2 T. extra-virgin olive oil
1 head cauliflower, chopped
10-oz. can marinated artichokes,
    drained and chopped
4 stalks celery with leaves,
    finely chopped
1/2 c. onion, finely chopped
3 cloves garlic, minced

2 T. fresh thyme leaves, chopped
salt and pepper to taste
2 T. all-purpose flour
3 c. chicken broth
2 c. half-and-half
Garnish: 1/2 c. shredded
    Parmesan cheese,
    3 T. chopped fresh parsley

In a large soup pot over medium heat, melt 2 tablespoons butter with
oil. Add cauliflower; cook for 5 minutes, stirring often. Add artichokes,
celery, onion, garlic and seasonings; cook for another 5 minutes. Push
vegetables to one side of the pot. Add remaining butter to other side
of pot; allow to melt and stir flour into butter. Cook and stir for one
minute. Add broth and half-and-half; stir together contents of pot.
Bring to a simmer over medium heat; cook until vegetables are fork-
tender. Purée soup with an immersion blender until still slightly
chunky. Garnish with Parmesan cheese and parsley. Makes 4 to
6 servings.

Top bowls of soup with crunchy cheese toasts. Cut bread with
a mini cookie cutter and brush lightly with olive oil. Broil on a
broiler pan for 2 to 3 minutes, until golden. Turn over and
sprinkle with freshly shredded Parmesan cheese. Broil another
2 to 3 minutes, until cheese melts. Yum!

Ella's Sauerkraut Soup

Jan Sherwood
Carpentersville, IL

*My sister Joanne shared this tasty recipe with me over 40 years ago,
and I enjoy it just as much now as I did way back then! Sometimes
I substitute crumbled crisp bacon or diced pork roast for the sausage.*

2 16-oz. pkgs. sauerkraut,
　 drained and rinsed
6 c. low-sodium beef broth
2 c. water
1 c. onion, chopped
6 T. butter

1 c. all-purpose flour
1 t. paprika
2 potatoes, peeled and diced
1 lb. Kielbasa sausage, diced
pepper to taste

Combine sauerkraut, broth and water in a large saucepan over medium
heat. Cover; simmer for 30 minutes. Meanwhile, in a Dutch oven over
medium heat, sauté onion in butter until translucent. Stir in flour and
paprika; cook and stir for 3 minutes. Add half of sauerkraut mixture to
Dutch oven; stir until smooth. Add remaining sauerkraut mixture and
potatoes. Reduce heat to low. Simmer for 30 minutes, stirring often. Add
sausage and pepper; simmer for 10 more minutes. Makes 6 servings.

Easy Buttermilk Rolls

Linda Rich
Bean Station, TN

*My mother made these cloverleaf rolls often...they are easy and
quick for yeast rolls. Only 90 minutes to make.*

2-3/4 c. all-purpose flour
2 T. sugar
1/2 t. baking soda
1/2 t. salt
1 env. quick-rise dry yeast

1 c. buttermilk, heated to
　 lukewarm
1/4 c. shortening
Garnish: melted butter

Combine flour, sugar, baking soda and salt; set aside. Add yeast to
buttermilk; stir in shortening. Add buttermilk mixture to flour mixture;
stir well. Let rise 45 minutes, or until double in bulk. Work down
dough and shape into small balls. Place in a greased muffin tin, adding
3 balls to each cup. Brush tops with melted butter. Let rise again until
double, about 30 minutes; Bake at 375 degrees for 20 to 30 minutes,
until golden. Makes one dozen.

Tastes-Like-Lasagna Soup

Beth Richter
Canby, MN

I started making this soup a few years back when I decided to go on a health kick. I wanted to make something that tasted good and was still good for me. Since I'm a big lasagna fan, it wasn't too hard for me to fall in love with this soup, but when even my nieces came back for seconds, I knew it was a hit!

1 lb. ground turkey
1/2 t. salt
seasoning salt to taste
32-oz. container chicken broth
15-oz. can tomato sauce
14-1/2 oz. can petite diced
    tomatoes

1-1/2 c. mini lasagna noodles,
    uncooked, or 4 lasagna
    noodles, uncooked and
    broken up
1/2 c. shredded mozzarella
    cheese
3 T. grated Parmesan cheese

Brown turkey in a large skillet over medium heat. Drain; season with salts. Add broth, tomato sauce and tomatoes with juice. Bring to a boil; reduce heat to low. Simmer, stirring occasionally, for about 20 minutes. Return to a boil; add noodles. Reduce heat to medium-low and simmer, uncovered, stirring occasionally, until noodles are tender and soup thickens slightly, 10 to 12 minutes. Remove from heat; stir in cheeses. Makes 4 to 6 servings.

Leftover soup? Ladle single portions into freezer bags...
seal, label and freeze. Then, when you need a quick-fix dinner,
simply let family members choose a bag, transfer soup to
a microwave-safe bowl and reheat.

Tuscan Tomato Soup

Carol Hickman
Kingsport, TN

My family likes to eat this soup when the weather turns cool. We curl up under blankets and sofa throws while watching a good movie together. Serve this with your favorite sandwich (it's delicious with grilled cheese!) or with bread or cheese sticks.

2 26-oz. cans tomato soup
12-oz. can evaporated milk
1-1/4 c. water
14-1/2 oz. can Italian-seasoned
   petite diced tomatoes
14-1/2 oz. can diced tomatoes
   with garlic and olive oil
2 T. Tuscan spice blend
1 T. Italian seasoning

1/4 t. red pepper flakes
salt and pepper to taste
1 t. sugar
1/2 c. grated Parmesan cheese
Garnish: additional grated
   Parmesan cheese
Optional: Italian-seasoned
   croutons

In a Dutch oven over medium-high heat, combine soup, evaporated milk and water. Whisk well until blended. Add both cans of tomatoes with juice, seasonings and sugar; stir well. Bring to a low boil. Increase heat to medium-low; stir in Parmesan cheese. Simmer for about 20 minutes, stirring occasionally. Top servings with additional Parmesan cheese and croutons, if desired. Makes 8 to 10 servings.

Turn a bowl of cream soup into spiderweb soup...fun for Halloween ! Spoon several tablespoons of sour cream into a plastic zipping bag. Snip off one corner and squeeze the sour cream in circles on the soup. To create a web effect, pull a toothpick across the circles, from the center to the edges.

Comforting Quesadillas

Barbara Imler
Noblesville, IN

These are a big hit at my house and are especially good with creamy tomato or potato soup. They're filled with good-for-you vegetables and pack a lot of flavor. This cooking method doesn't require flipping them, so you won't make a mess with lost fillings...the cheese helps act like "glue" to hold all the good stuff inside.

2 t. canola or olive oil
1 red, orange or yellow pepper,
   sliced
1 sweet onion, sliced
1 clove garlic, thinly sliced
4 10-inch flour tortillas
1 c. shredded Cheddar cheese,
   divided

1 to 2 5-oz. cans chicken,
   drained and divided
1 roma tomato, chopped and
   divided
Optional: jalapeño slices, black
   beans, corn, sliced black
   olives
Garnish: sour cream, salsa

Add oil to a large skillet over medium heat. Add pepper and onion; cook and stir to desired tenderness. Add garlic just before vegetables are done; cook for one more minute. Remove vegetables to a bowl. Turn heat to medium-low; add a little more oil to skillet if needed. Place one tortilla in skillet; cook for one minute. Sprinkle with 1/4 cup cheese; cook until bottom is crisp and golden. Remove tortilla to a cutting board; set aside. Turn heat to low. Place second tortilla in pan; sprinkle with 1/4 cup cheese. Top with half each of pepper mixture, chicken and tomato. Add any optional ingredients desired. Place first tortilla cheese-side down over the top; press lightly. Cook until bottom of second tortilla is golden. Slide quesadilla onto a cutting board. Repeat process with remaining ingredients to make another quesadilla. With a pizza cutter, slice each quesadilla into 6 wedges. Serve with sour cream and salsa. Makes 4 servings.

For a quick and casual centerpiece,
curl a string of dried chile peppers into
a circle, then set a hurricane with a
fat red candle in the center.

Muffuletta Sliders

Dana Cunningham
Lafayette, LA

These tasty little sandwiches are easy to make ahead...perfect for tailgating parties! I like to garnish each slider with a small whole olive or tiny sweet pickle, skewered with a festive party pick.

2 16-oz. jars pickled mixed vegetables, drained
3/4 c. chopped green olives with pimentos, drained
2 T. olive oil & vinegar salad dressing

12 slider rolls, split
6 slices Swiss cheese, cut in half
12 thin slices deli baked ham
12 slices deli Genoa salami
6 slices provolone cheese, cut in half

Add pickled vegetables to a food processor or blender. Process just until finely chopped. Transfer to a bowl; stir in olives and salad dressing. Separate rolls; spoon vegetable mixture generously over cut side of each roll bottom. Layer each roll bottom with 1/2 slice Swiss cheese, one slice ham, one slice salami and 1/2 slice provolone cheese. Add tops of rolls; arrange sliders on a serving tray. Serve immediately, or cover with plastic wrap and chill until serving time. Makes one dozen.

Tuck a tiny American flag toothpick into sandwiches! Not only fun, they're great for holding together overstuffed sandwiches.

Hoagie Dip for Sandwiches

Phyllis Rack
Hollman Estates, IL

You'll be amazed how much this delicious spread tastes like a hoagie sandwich! This makes a lot, so feel free to halve the recipe. Sure to be a hit at parties.

1/2 lb. deli salami, diced
1/2 lb. deli boiled ham, diced
1/2 lb. American cheese, diced
1 c. lettuce, shredded
3/4 c. tomato, diced
1/4 c. onion, diced
1 c. mayonnaise
1 T. dried oregano
salt and pepper to taste
sliced Italian bread

In a large bowl, combine all ingredients except bread; mix well. Cover and keep refrigerated. If making ahead, add lettuce and tomato at serving time. Serve as a spread on slices of Italian bread. Makes 12 servings.

Easy Pimento Cheese

Janet New
Bronston, KY

My cousin gave me this recipe because she knew how much my husband loves pimento cheese. It is so easy to make and being homemade makes it even tastier. When I make this recipe, he always thanks her for sharing it and brags that it's the best he's ever had!

8-oz. pkg. cream cheese, softened
8-oz. pkg. pasteurized process cheese, softened
1/2 c. sweet relish, drained
2 to 3 T. mayonnaise-style salad dressing
2-oz. jar sliced pimentos, drained
sliced bread

In a bowl, mix cheeses together until blended smoothly. Add remaining ingredients except bread. Blend well; do not overmix. Cover; keep refrigerated. Serve as a spread on slices of bread. Makes 6 to 8 servings.

We all have hometown appetites.

–Clementine Paddleford

Easy But Elegant Chicken Salad

Anita Mullins
Eldridge, MO

This is a last-minute recipe I came up with for my granddaughter's birthday. I stopped to pick up canned chicken, then tossed it together and made finger sandwiches. It was a huge hit and was requested for another grandchild's birthday a few weeks later! No matter how much I make, I never have leftovers.

2 to 3 6-oz. cans chicken,
   drained and flaked
1/4 c. sweetened dried
   cranberries, chopped

1 stalk celery, finely chopped
1/4 c. pecans, finely minced
1 c. mayonnaise, or to taste
Optional: bread, lettuce leaves

Combine all ingredients except bread or lettuce in a bowl; mix well. For the best flavor, cover and refrigerate overnight before serving. Spread on bread for finger sandwiches, or serve on lettuce leaves as a salad. Makes 4 to 6 servings.

Headed for a picnic? Pack favorite sandwich fillings into covered containers to tuck in the cooler. Assemble sandwiches at your picnic site...so convenient, and no more soggy bread!

Baked Cuban-Style Sandwiches
Cheri Maxwell
Gulf Breeze, FL

Your family & friends will love these hot, hearty sandwiches...
they're just a little different!

2 t. honey
1 t. water
1 sheet frozen puff pastry
  dough, thawed
4 t. mustard
8 thin slices deli baked ham

8 thin slices Swiss cheese
8 thin slices deli roast pork
4 sandwich-style slices kosher
  dill pickle
2 t. sesame seed

Stir together honey and water in a cup; set aside. Unfold pastry sheet on a floured surface; roll out into a 12-inch square. Cut pastry into 4, 6-inch squares. Spread each square with one teaspoon mustard, leaving a 1/2-inch border around the edge. Layer each square with 2 slices ham, 2 slices cheese, one slice pickle and 2 slices pork. Brush edges of pastry with honey mixture. Fold pastry diagonally over filling to form a triangle; crimp with a fork to seal. Brush filled pastries with remaining honey mixture; sprinkle with sesame seed. Place on an ungreased baking sheet. Bake at 400 degrees for 20 minutes, or until hot and golden. Set baking sheet on a wire rack for 5 minutes before serving. Makes 4 servings.

Pick up a dozen pint-size Mason jars. They're perfect for serving cold beverages at casual get-togethers.

Everybody's Favorite Ham Sandwiches

Nancy Girard
Chesapeake, VA

Men go crazy for these sandwiches! This is the recipe that everybody asks me for. They're assembled the night before, so they're full of buttery goodness. Try it...you'll be handing out copies too!

1 c. butter, sliced
1/4 c. onion, minced
1/4 c. brown sugar, packed
2 T. poppy seed
2 T. spicy mustard
1 T. Worcestershire sauce

1/2 t. garlic powder
1 T. fresh parsley, chopped
24 small dinner rolls, halved
mayonnaise to taste
24 thin slices deli baked ham
24 thin slices Swiss cheese

For butter marinade, melt butter in a skillet over medium heat. Add onion; sauté until soft. Add brown sugar, poppy seed, mustard, Worcestershire sauce and garlic powder. Cook and stir until brown sugar is dissolved. Remove from heat; stir in parsley and set aside. Spread cut side of bun bottoms with a thin layer of mayonnaise. Top each bun bottom with one slice ham and one slice cheese, folding to fit buns. Replace bun tops. Divide filled buns between 2 aluminum foil-lined 13"x9" baking pans. Pour butter marinade evenly over both pans of buns. Cover tightly with foil; refrigerate overnight. Bake, covered, at 350 degrees for 25 minutes. Remove foil; bake an additional 10 minutes. Makes 24 mini sandwiches.

Make up some handy file cards listing the ingredients needed for your most-used party recipes. Shopping will be a breeze!

Tastiest Shredded Chicken

Peggy Market
Elida, OH

This recipe comes in so handy when you need a quick and very tasty sandwich. All of the ingredients can be kept in your pantry. The best part is that it can be served as a sandwich filling or as a salad on a cold plate with sliced tomatoes and cottage cheese. Either way, it goes very quickly!

10-3/4 oz. can cream of chicken soup
2 c. regular or low-sodium chicken broth, divided
2 13-oz. cans chicken breast, drained and shredded

2 to 3 c. herb-seasoned stuffing mix
Optional: sliced bread

In a large saucepan over medium heat, whisk together soup and one cup broth. Add chicken with juices and 2 cups dressing mix; stir well. Reduce heat to low. Cook, stirring often, for about 10 minutes. Add more broth as needed to keep mixture moistened on the bottom. Additional dressing mix may be added to desired consistency. Cook until mixture is hot and bubbly. Spoon mixture onto bread to make sandwiches, or scoop and serve as a salad plate. Makes 8 to 10 servings.

Mini versions of favorite hot sandwiches are so appealing...diners with light appetites can take just one, while those with heartier tastes can sample two or three. Try using small slider buns or brown & serve dinner rolls instead of full-size buns.

Chicken Croquettes & Dill Sauce

Teresa Eller
Kansas City, KS

*My husband doesn't care for salmon patties, so I came up
with this version of the croquette. We both love it!*

13-oz. can chicken, drained
   and flaked
1/4 c. mayonnaise
2 eggs, beaten
1/2 c. onion, diced
3 stalks celery, diced
1/4 c. grated Parmesan cheese
1/4 c. all-purpose flour

1 t. garlic powder
1 t. mustard
1/2 t. chili powder
1 c. Italian-seasoned dry bread
   crumbs, divided
1 T. canola oil
4 ciabatta rolls, split
softened butter to taste

In a bowl, combine chicken, mayonnaise, eggs, onion, celery, cheese,
flour, seasonings and 3/4 cup bread crumbs. Mix well; let stand for
10 to 15 minutes. Form into 4 balls; flatten to make patties. Place
remaining bread crumbs in a shallow dish; coat patties on both sides.
Heat oil in a skillet over medium heat. Add patties; cook until coating
is crisp and golden on both sides. Transfer patties to a lightly greased
8"x8" baking pan. Cover; bake at 350 degrees for 30 to 40 minutes.
Serve croquettes on toasted, buttered rolls, topped with desired amount
of Dill Sauce. Makes 4 sandwiches.

Dill Sauce:

8-oz. pkg. cream cheese,
   softened, or 8-oz. container
   sour cream
1 T. dill weed

1 T. garlic powder
1 T. onion powder
1 T. chili powder
1 T. celery salt

Blend all ingredients in a bowl until well mixed. Cover; keep
refrigerated. Use as a sandwich topping and dip.

Stir caramel topping into a mug of hot
cider for an instant warmer-upper.

Chipotle Stadium Burgers

Athena Colegrove
Big Springs, TX

Ramp up your tailgating cook-out with these zesty burgers! Garnish with a dollop of chipotle mayonnaise, sliced avocado and a sprig of cilantro. Sure to score a touchdown!

1 lb. ground beef
1/2 c. onion, minced
2 T. fresh cilantro, chopped
1 canned chipotle chile in adobo
   sauce, minced
1 t. garlic powder
1 t. onion powder

1 t. seasoned salt
1/4 t. pepper
4 slices Pepper Jack or Monterey
   Jack cheese
1 T. olive oil, divided
4 hamburger buns, split

In a bowl, combine all ingredients except cheese, oil and buns. Mix well; form into 4 patties. Heat a grill to medium-high heat; lightly brush grate with some of the oil. Add patties and cook to desired doneness, about 4 minutes per side. Remove patties to a plate. Top with cheese slices; set aside. Meanwhile, brush remaining oil over cut sides of buns. Grill cut sides of buns for one to 2 minutes. until toasted. Serve patties on buns. Makes 4 sandwiches.

Invite friends over for a cookout before the big game. Begin with invitations made of felt in the shape of pennants or use a permanent marker to write party information on small plastic footballs.

Pepperoni Pizza Burgers

Janice Woods
Northern Cambria, PA

My family just loves pizza and burgers, so this makes for
a great change at mealtime.

1-1/2 lbs. lean ground beef
1/2 lb. Italian ground pork
  sausage
1/2 t. Italian seasoning
12 slices mozzarella and/or
  provolone cheese

3-oz. pkg. sliced pepperoni
6 kaiser rolls, split
softened butter to taste
3/4 c. marinara or pizza sauce,
  warmed
grated Parmesan cheese to taste

In a large bowl, combine beef, sausage and seasoning. Mix well; form
into 6 patties. Heat a large skillet over medium-high heat. Add patties
and cook to desired doneness, about 4 minutes per side. Reduce heat
to low. When patties are nearly done, top each patty with 2 slices
cheese and 5 to 6 slices pepperoni. Cover skillet; continue cooking until
done, cheese is melted and pepperoni is warmed through. Spread cut
sides of rolls with softened butter. In a separate skillet over medium
heat, toast rolls until crisp and golden. Spread cut sides of rolls with
sauce; sprinkle with Parmesan cheese. Place patties on bun bottoms;
add tops. Serve immediately. Makes 6 sandwiches.

A little "magic" for the kids! Put a drop of green food coloring
into their milk glasses, then fill with milk as you tap
the glasses with a magic wand.

Root Beer Pulled Chicken

Megan Brooks
Antioch, TN

When we went to a cookout at my Aunt Betty's house, she served these delicious sandwiches. I asked her what the secret ingredient was...couldn't believe it when she told me it was root beer! If you can't find boneless chicken thighs, no problem...the bones will be very easy to remove when the chicken is cooked.

2-1/2 lbs. boneless, skinless
   chicken thighs
2 t. seasoned salt
12-oz. can root beer (not diet)
1 T. oil
1/2 c. onion, chopped
1 c. catsup
1/4 c. brown sugar, packed
1/4 c. molasses
2 T. mustard
2 t. smoke-flavored cooking
   sauce
10 sesame sandwich buns, split
Garnish: favorite coleslaw

Spray a 4 to 6-quart slow cooker with non-stick vegetable spray. Sprinkle chicken with seasoned salt; add to slow cooker. Pour root beer over chicken. Cover and cook on high setting for 5 to 6 hours, until chicken is very tender. About 30 minutes before serving time, heat oil in a large saucepan over medium-high heat. Sauté onion until golden, about 5 minutes; drain. Stir in remaining ingredients except buns and coleslaw. Reduce heat to low. Simmer for 10 minutes, stirring occasionally. When chicken is done, remove to a plate. Drain slow cooker, reserving 1/2 cup of cooking liquid. Shred chicken; add to sauce in saucepan along with reserved cooking liquid. Simmer gently until heated through. Top each roll with 1/2 cup chicken mixture and a spoonful of coleslaw. Makes 10 sandwiches.

Whip up some cozy throws of colorful fleece...perfect for football games, hayrides and snoozing on the sofa. Simply snip fringe all around the edges. They're so easy, you can make one for each member of the family in no time at all!

Skinny French Dip Beef Sandwiches

Marian Forck
Chamois, MO

My daughter Sarah gave me this recipe to try and we loved it.
The slow-cooked beef is perfect for stuffing into crusty
bread for sandwiches.

2-lb. lean beef roast
14-1/2 oz. can beef broth
1/2 c. water
1 onion, sliced
2 cloves garlic, sliced

3 T. soy sauce
1 T. dried thyme, minced
1 t. dried rosemary
1 t. pepper
6 to 8 crusty hard rolls, split

Slice roast into several pieces; trim any excess fat. Place roast in a 4-quart slow cooker; pour in broth and water. Top with remaining ingredients except rolls. Cover and cook on low setting for 9 to 10 hours, until roast is very tender. Shred roast with a fork; spoon into rolls. Serve with cooking juices from slow cooker for dipping. Makes 6 to 8 sandwiches.

Fill up a relish tray with crunchy fresh veggies as a simple side dish...add a cup of this creamy dip. Combine one cup cottage cheese, 1/4 cup plain yogurt, one tablespoon minced onion, one teaspoon dried parsley and 1/4 teaspoon dill weed. Blend until smooth and chill before serving.

Mom's Bar-B-Ques

Sharon Leach
Two Rivers, WI

My mom started making these yummy sandwiches way back in the 1950s. I think the recipe may have come from the back of the soup can. She always served these at my birthday parties. Sometimes I'll change it up by omitting the water and using tomato soup instead of chicken gumbo. It's good either way.

1 lb. ground beef
1/2 c. onion, chopped
10-3/4 oz. can chicken gumbo
   soup
1/2 c. plus 2 T. water

3 T. mustard, or to taste
3 T. catsup, or to taste
1/8 t. pepper
sandwich buns, split

In a skillet over medium heat, brown beef with onion. Drain; stir in remaining ingredients except buns. Bring to a boil; reduce heat to medium-low. Simmer for 10 to 20 minutes, stirring occasionally. Serve beef mixture spooned onto buns. Makes 6 sandwiches.

My husband used to be the cook at our church camp. Every fall, at the end of the busy summer season, all of the employees and their families would gather at the director's house for a cookout. Grilled hamburgers, hot dogs and corn, sides and desserts... there were too many dishes to count, much less eat them all. We would end the celebration around the bonfire toasting marshmallows and making s'mores. Such fun!

–Marsha Brown, Okmulgee, OK

Dip-Dip Roast Beef Sandwiches

Rebecca McKeich
Palm Beach Gardens, FL

My husband brought this easy weeknight recipe into our marriage and it is now a family favorite.

1-oz. pkg. au jus gravy mix
3 c. cold water
1 lb. thinly sliced deli roast beef

4 hoagie rolls, partially split
 and opened up
8 slices provolone cheese

In a large microwave-safe bowl, whisk together au jus mix and cold water. Add roast beef slices to au jus, one a time. Microwave on high for 5 minutes. Meanwhile, broil rolls, cut-side up, until lightly toasted. Remove from oven; heap hot roast beef evenly on one side of each roll. Top beef on each roll with 2 folded slices of cheese. Return rolls to broiler until cheese is melted; close sandwiches. Serve with remaining au jus for dipping. Makes 4 sandwiches.

Barbecued Worm Sandwiches

Donna Wilson
Maryville, TN

I enjoy making this for my kids at Halloween! The hot dogs curl up to look like worms when cooked and they love that.

8 hot dogs, cut lengthwise into
 6 strips each
1/2 c. barbecue sauce

8 sandwich buns, split
8 slices favorite cheese

Spray a skillet with non-stick vegetable spray. Add hot dog strips; cook until browned. Stir in barbecue sauce; toss to coat until bubbly. Spoon hot dog mixture onto buns; top with a slice of cheese. Makes 8 sandwiches.

On chilly evenings, welcome guests with a warming beverage... great for a tailgating thermos too. In a kettle, combine a 48-ounce bottle of vegetable cocktail juice with 4 cans of beef broth. (Choose low-sodium versions if you like.) Simmer until heated through and serve in big mugs.

Sally's Chicken Packets

*Kathy Courington
Canton, GA*

My best friend Sally gave me this recipe years ago and the kids really loved it. Very kid-friendly! Always a favorite in our house. It's a great way to use leftover chicken or turkey.

2 c. cooked chicken, chopped
3-oz. pkg. cream cheese,
  softened
2 T. milk
1 T. fresh chives, chopped
salt to taste

2 8-oz. tubes refrigerated
  crescent rolls
1/4 c. butter, melted
1/2 c. seasoned croutons,
  crushed

In a bowl, mix together chicken, cream cheese, milk, chives and salt; set aside. Separate crescents into 8 squares, pressing dough along perforated lines to seal. Spoon 1/4 cup chicken mixture onto each square. Fold over to form rectangles; press closed with a fork. Dip packets into melted butter and then into crushed croutons. Arrange packets on an ungreased baking sheet. Bake at 350 degrees for 20 to 30 minutes, until golden. Serve warm. Chicken filling may be made ahead of time, wrapped and frozen. To prepare, thaw overnight in the refrigerator. Makes 8 servings.

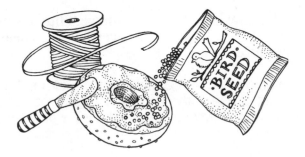

Let the kids whip up some birdseed bagels for the birds as the weather turns chilly. Just spread peanut butter on the cut side of a bagel; coat with birdseed. Slip a length of twine in the bagel hole and hang from a tree.

Harvest Moon
Sides & Salads

Bell Pepper Slaw

April Garner
Independence, KY

The flavor of this very colorful slaw is best when made a day before serving...convenient for potlucks and parties!

10-oz. pkg. angel hair shredded
   coleslaw
5 assorted peppers (green,
   red, orange, yellow and/or
   purple), thinly sliced
1 c. red and/or yellow cherry
   tomatoes, halved
3/4 c. zesty Italian salad
   dressing

1/4 c. sweet balsamic salad
   dressing
1 T. sugar
1 t. dried basil
1 t. dried oregano
1 t. kosher salt

Combine coleslaw, peppers and tomatoes in a large glass bowl. Stir to combine; set aside. In a small bowl, combine remaining ingredients. Whisk well and pour over coleslaw mixture; toss to coat. For the best flavor, cover and refrigerate overnight. Makes 12 servings.

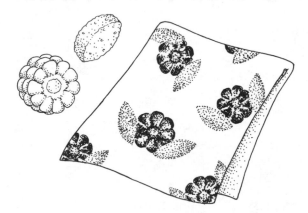

Make a corncob printed tablecloth...fun for kids to do! Cut or break an ear of dried corn in half to reveal a flower shape. Pour fabric paint in a paper plate and stamp on a plain tablecloth. Leaves may be added with a shape cut from a kitchen sponge.

Zesty Black Bean Salad

Tricia Roberson
King George, VA

As a military wife, I have moved around quite a bit and have been lucky enough to experience all different types of cultural cooking. We live in Virginia and were stationed in Texas. How I miss Texas! I try to infuse some of the wonderful flavors I enjoyed often in Texas into my cooking. My family, even my picky 16-year-old daughter, wolfed down this salad with chips and it was gone before dinner was on the table.

14-1/2 oz. can seasoned black
    beans, drained and rinsed
10-oz. pkg. frozen corn, thawed
1 green pepper, chopped
1/2 c. grape tomatoes, chopped

1/4 c. onion, chopped
2 T. sweet-hot pepper relish
1/2 c. zesty lime salad dressing
tortilla chips

In a serving bowl, combine vegetables and relish; mix well. Drizzle with salad dressing; toss to coat well. Let stand 30 minutes, or cover and refrigerate until serving time. Serve with tortilla chips. Makes 4 to 6 servings.

Indian summer days can be warm, even though it's fall. When heading to a tailgating get-together, keep traveling salads crisp by packing them in an ice-filled cooler. At serving time, scoop some of the cooler ice into a bowl and set the salad bowls right on top. Nestle them into the ice a bit to keep them cool.

Crisp Apple-Onion Salad

Goreta Brown
Alberta, Canada

This is our all-time favorite salad, very tasty and easy to make. I like to triple the recipe and keep the leftover dressing in the fridge so that I can make it several times during the week. My husband and I are blue cheese lovers, but soft goat cheese can be used instead.

10-oz. pkg. mixed salad greens
1/2 red onion, sliced
1/2 apple, cored and thinly
   sliced

1/4 c. sweetened dried
   cranberries
1/4 c. crumbled blue cheese

Make Dijon Dressing ahead of time; refrigerate. In a large salad bowl, combine greens, onion and apple. Drizzle with dressing; toss salad with dressing. Add cranberries and cheese; toss gently to mix. Serve immediately. Makes 4 servings.

Dijon Dressing:

2 T. olive oil
1-1/2 T. cider vinegar
1 T. Dijon mustard

1 T. sugar
salt and pepper to taste

Combine all ingredients in a jar. Cover and shake well. Keep refrigerated.

Paint names on colorful mini gourds for whimsical placecards.

Light Apple Waldorf Salad

Janet Sharp
Milford, OH

*If you like Waldorf salad, you will enjoy this healthy lighter version.
It is especially delicious with pork tenderloin.*

10-oz. pkg. romaine lettuce or
   fresh spinach
2 apples, cored and sliced

1 c. seedless grapes, halved
1 c. celery, sliced
1 c. walnut halves, toasted

Combine all salad ingredients in bowl. Just before serving, pour desired amount of Red Wine Vinegar Dressing over salad. Toss well and serve immediately. Makes 4 servings.

Red Wine Vinegar Dressing:

1/2 c. olive oil
1/4 c. red wine vinegar

salt and pepper to taste

Shake ingredients well in a covered jar or process well in a blender. Keep refrigerated.

Toasting really brings out the flavor of shelled nuts. Place nuts in a small dry skillet. Cook and stir over low heat for a few minutes, until toasty and golden...it's that simple!

Diane's Potato Salad

Christine Wheeler
Jupiter, FL

*A friend of mine uses this recipe when she caters. It is easy
to make and so delicious...my family loves it!*

5 lbs. redskin potatoes, cooked
    and cubed
8 to 12 eggs, hard-boiled, peeled
    and chopped
1 lb. bacon, crisply cooked and
    crumbled

1 to 2 bunches green onions,
    chopped
16-oz. jar mayonnaise
16-oz. jar mayonnaise-style
    salad dressing
salt and pepper to taste

In a large serving bowl, combine potatoes, eggs, bacon and onions;
set aside. In a separate bowl, combine remaining ingredients. Gently
fold mayonnaise mixture into potato mixture. Cover and chill at least
2 hours before serving. Makes 10 to 12 servings.

Every Thanksgiving my family would go to my Aunt Madeline's
farm to celebrate the day. One year my older cousins decided to
have our own Thanksgiving parade. We dressed up as Indians
and Pilgrims and sat on hay bales on the wagons which were
pulled by tractors. My grandfather was the big Indian chief. The
adults came outside and lined the long driveway waving as they
laughed and cheered. It was a lot of fun...I will never forget
our days on my aunt's farm.

-Donna Weidner, Schaumburg, IL

Bacon & Broccoli Salad

Leona Krivda
Belle Vernon, PA

This salad is full of tasty ingredients...great to take to a picnic or any get-together. I always make it for Thanksgiving because if I didn't, I would hear about it from my family!

8 slices bacon, crisply cooked
   and crumbled
1 bunch broccoli, cut into
   bite-size flowerets
1/2 head cauliflower, cut into
   bite-size flowerets

1 c. Cheddar cheese, shredded
   or diced
1/2 c. purple onion, finely
   chopped
2 T. sunflower seed kernels

Make Cider Vinegar Dressing the day before; refrigerate. In a salad bowl, combine all the ingredients; mix well. Pour dressing over salad. Toss very well to coat evenly. Cover and refrigerate until serving time. Makes 8 to 10 servings.

Cider Vinegar Dressing:

3/4 c. mayonnaise-style salad
   dressing

3 T. cider vinegar
1/3 c. sugar

Combine all ingredients. Mix well; cover and refrigerate.

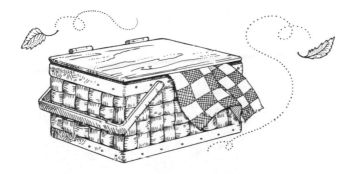

Get ready for spur-of-the-moment picnics on sunny autumn days! Tuck a basket filled with picnic supplies into the car trunk along with a quilt to sit on.

Antipasto Rotini Salad

JoAnn
Gooseberry Patch

This flavorful, colorful salad has become a favorite at our annual block party. Sometimes I'll dress it up even more with rainbow rotini and half green, half red pepper slices.

3 c. rotini pasta, uncooked
2 c. broccoli flowerets
1/4 lb. thinly sliced deli Genoa salami, cut into strips
15-oz. can red kidney beans, drained and rinsed
4 roma tomatoes, cut into thin wedges
1 green pepper, sliced
1/2 red onion, sliced
1/2 c. sliced black olives, drained

Cook pasta according to package directions, adding broccoli during last 3 minutes of cooking time. Drain; rinse with cold water and set aside. In a large serving bowl, combine pasta mixture with remaining ingredients. Drizzle with Parmesan-Pepper Dressing; toss until well mixed. Cover and refrigerate at least 2 hours. Stir again before serving. Makes 18 to 20 servings.

Peppered Parmesan Dressing:

3/4 c. Italian salad dressing
1/2 c. shredded Parmesan cheese
1-1/2 t. coarse pepper
1/2 t. Worcestershire sauce
3 cloves garlic, minced

Combine all ingredients in a bowl; whisk well.

Give favorite pasta recipes a twist for fall...pick up some pasta in seasonal shapes like autumn leaves or pumpkins! Some even come in veggie colors like orange, red or green.

Grandmother's German Potato Salad

Judy Scherer
Benton, MO

My grandmother often made this potato salad and I always requested it, even for my birthday! When I asked her for the recipe, she said, "It takes a little of this & a little of that." Finally she gave me a little bit of recipe to go by. I got to make my version of it just once for her. She tasted it and gave me pointers on how to make it better. I hope you'll enjoy it as much as I do!

5 lbs. potatoes, peeled
1 white onion, sliced or diced
1 lb. bacon
salt and pepper to taste

1 c. cider vinegar
1-1/2 c. sugar
3 to 3-1/2 T. cornstarch
Optional: diced green onion

In a kettle, cover potatoes with water. Cook over medium-high heat until fork-tender; drain. Slice or cube potatoes; return to pan. Add onion and set aside. Meanwhile, cook bacon in a skillet over medium heat until crisp. Pour crumbled bacon and drippings over warm potato mixture; mix well. Season with salt and pepper; set aside. In a saucepan, combine vinegar, sugar and cornstarch. Cook and stir over medium-low heat until thickened. Pour over potato mixture; stir well. Garnish with green onion, if using. May be served warm or cold. Makes 8 to 10 servings.

ooompah!

On a sunny autumn day, throw a backyard Oktoberfest party! Set a festive mood with polka music. Toss some brats on the grill to serve in hard rolls, topped with sauerkraut. Round out the menu with potato salad, homemade applesauce and German chocolate cake for dessert. Sure to be fun for all!

Mom's Ten-Vegetable Salad

Debra Caraballo
Manahawkin, NJ

This is one of my mom's recipes that she made for nearly every get-together we attended. It actually has only nine vegetables...the tenth has always remained a mystery! The leftovers taste even better the next day.

1 c. celery, diced
1 onion, halved and sliced
1 green pepper, diced
15-oz. can green peas, drained
15-oz. can shoepeg corn, drained
14-1/2 oz. can sliced carrots, drained

14-1/2 oz. can French-cut green beans, drained
8-oz. can sliced water chestnuts, drained
2-oz. jar sliced pimentos

Combine all ingredients in a large serving bowl. Pour desired amount of Marinade over vegetables; toss to mix well. Let cool; cover and refrigerate overnight for the best flavor. Makes 10 to 12 servings.

Marinade:

1-1/2 c. sugar
1 T. salt
1 c. oil

1 c. white vinegar
1/2 c. water
1 t. pepper

Combine all ingredients in a saucepan over medium heat. Bring to a boil; cook and stir until sugar dissolves.

For tailgating spreads, serve up colorful salads in clear plastic cups. So easy for everyone to serve themselves, and clean-up is a snap!

Kicked-Up Corn Salad

Beckie Apple
Grannis, AR

My whole family loves corn with any meal! I especially like this salad recipe because it is served chilled. It uses canned corn, so it can be made year 'round.

3 15-oz. cans corn, drained
2 green onions, chopped
1/4 c. bacon bits, or more
   to taste
1 c. shredded Cheddar cheese

1/4 c. mayonnaise
1/8 t. salt
1/8 t. pepper
1/8 t. red pepper flakes
3 c. chili cheese corn chips

Mix all ingredients except corn chips in a large serving bowl; stir well. Cover and refrigerate for 2 to 3 hours. Fold in chips when ready to serve. Makes 6 to 8 servings.

Kyle's Cornbread

Lynnette Jones
East Flat Rock, NC

Our grown son is a fabulous chef and has many recipes of his own. This cornbread is one of our favorites. Not only is it good with vegetables and soups, it's scrumptious topped with honey or jam.

1 c. medium-grind cornmeal
1 c. all-purpose flour
3 T. brown sugar, packed
2 t. baking powder
1 t. baking soda

1 t. salt
2 eggs, beaten
1/2 c. oil
1 c. buttermilk

In a large bowl, combine cornmeal, flour, brown sugar, baking powder, baking soda and salt; mix well. Add eggs, oil and buttermilk. Stir until combined. Pour batter into a well greased 8" cast-iron skillet. Bake at 400 degrees for 30 to 35 minutes. Cut into squares. Makes 8 servings.

All seasons sweet, but autumn best of all.

-Elinor Wylie

Ultimate Greek Salad

Janis Parr
Ontario, Canada

This amazing salad is full of everything good for you and the homemade dressing is the finishing touch!

1 cucumber, sliced lengthwise and cubed
2 tomatoes, cut into wedges
1/2 green pepper, cut into chunks
1/2 red pepper, cut into chunks
1/2 yellow pepper, cut into chunks
1/2 red onion, sliced
2 c. crumbled feta cheese
1 c. sliced black olives, drained
salt and pepper to taste

To a large salad bowl, add vegetables in order listed. Season with salt and pepper; toss gently. Cover and refrigerate until well chilled. At serving time, pour desired amount of Salad Dressing over salad; toss gently. Makes 6 servings.

Salad Dressing:

3/4 c. extra-virgin olive oil
1/4 c. grapeseed or corn oil
1/2 c. cider vinegar
1 T. brown sugar, packed
1/2 t. Dijon mustard

Combine all ingredients in a bowl; whisk together until brown sugar dissolves. Keep refrigerated.

For the easiest-ever fall centerpiece, simply lay a wreath of autumn leaves or bittersweet berries on the table and set a pumpkin in the center...so clever!

Tom's Turnip Slaw

Thomas Hiegel
Union City, OH

I love slaw, but it seems like there was always something missing. I worked a long time until I came up with this recipe. To me, it is just right and it is now my favorite. I hope it'll become yours too!

2 c. white turnips, peeled
   and shredded
2 c. cabbage, shredded
1/2 c. carrot, peeled and
   shredded
1/4 c. red pepper, finely chopped
1/4 c. onion, finely chopped

1/4 c. mayonnaise
2 T. vinegar
2 T. sugar
1 t. prepared horseradish
1/4 t. salt
1/4 t. cayenne pepper

In a large serving bowl, combine all vegetables; toss to mix and set aside. In a small bowl, blend remaining ingredients. Add mayonnaise mixture to vegetable mixture; mix well. Cover and refrigerate. Makes 6 to 8 servings.

Fall mums come in glorious shades of red, yellow and orange... you can't have too many! Tuck pots into hollowed-out pumpkins to march up the porch steps.

Taffy Apple Salad

Sharry Murawski
Oak Forest, IL

I bring this salad to every potluck I am invited to. It is a big hit wherever I take it! I can always count on coming home with an empty bowl. I have shared this recipe with numerous friends.

2 8-oz. cans crushed pineapple
1 c. sugar
2 T. all-purpose flour
2 eggs, lightly beaten
4 t. vinegar

7 to 8 Granny Smith apples, peeled, cored and chopped
2 8-oz. containers frozen whipped topping, thawed
1-1/2 c. salted roasted peanuts

In a saucepan, combine pineapple with juice, sugar, flour, eggs and vinegar. Cook over low heat, stirring constantly, until mixture is thickened and sugar is dissolved. Transfer mixture to a large serving bowl; cover and refrigerate overnight. Add apples to cooled pineapple mixture; mix well. Fold in whipped topping and peanuts. Serve immediately, or cover and chill. Makes 15 servings.

Have fun apple picking with your children! To help little ones reach up into the trees, cut a 2-liter soda bottle in half around the middle. Tuck a broomstick into the spout and tape together. Just tap an apple gently and it should drop right into the bottle scoop.

Awesome Grape Salad

Kris Couchman
Centerville, IA

This salad is sweet, creamy and addictive! I got the recipe from my sister-in-law when she brought it to a family get-together. After one taste, I put it on my list of top three favorite salads. I make it for special occasions because even the hardest-to-please person will absolutely love it. If you think this makes too much, you'll be surprised how fast it disappears. Everyone wants seconds!

8-oz. container sour cream
8-oz. pkg. cream cheese,
   softened
1/2 c. sugar
1 t. vanilla extract, or to taste

2 lbs. seedless green grapes
2 lbs. seedless red grapes
1 c. brown sugar, packed
1 c. crushed pecans, or to taste

In a large serving bowl, stir together sour cream, cream cheese, sugar and vanilla until blended. Stir in grapes. For topping, combine brown sugar and pecans. Sprinkle over grape mixture to cover completely. Cover and chill overnight. Serves 12 to 15.

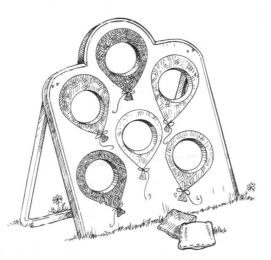

Show your hometown spirit...cheer on the high school football team with a Friday neighborhood block party. Invite neighbors to bring along their favorite dish to share...don't forget a game of beanbag toss for the kids!

Sunshine Salad

Glenna Kennedy
Ontario, Canada

An oldie but goodie that I have been making for more than 25 years. It is a great gelatin salad to make for the holidays. Most kids don't like jellied salads with veggies in them. This one is very different and kids love it!

1 c. orange juice
2 envs. unflavored gelatin
1/4 c. sugar
1/2 t. salt
juice of 2 lemons

14-oz. can pineapple chunks, drained and juice reserved
1 c. carrots, peeled and grated
1/2 c. celery, thinly sliced
10-oz. can mandarin oranges

Pour orange juice into a saucepan over low heat; sprinkle with gelatin. Cook and stir until gelatin dissolves, about 4 minutes. Pour mixture into a large bowl. Add sugar, salt, lemon juice and reserved pineapple juice. Stir well until sugar is dissolved. Chill for about 10 minutes. Cut pineapple chunks into smaller pieces, if desired. Add pineapple to gelatin mixture along with carrots, celery and undrained oranges. If desired, pour gelatin mixture into a fancy 10-cup gelatin mold. Cover and chill for several hours, until set. At serving time, if using a mold, let stand at room temperature for several minutes. Turn out onto a plate. Makes 8 to 10 servings.

At country potlucks and carry-ins, fruity gelatin salads are yummy when topped with a dollop of creamy lemon mayonnaise. Stir 3 tablespoons each of lemon juice, light cream and powdered sugar into 1/2 cup mayonnaise. Garnish with a sprinkle of lemon zest, if you like.

Doug's Favorite Fruit Salad

Joan Chance
Houston, TX

My son-in-law is leery of my cooking as I like to try new recipes. However, this is one he really liked, so I named it after him. Sugar-free puddings are fine, if you prefer.

29-oz. can peach slices
20-oz. can pineapple chunks
3.4-oz. pkg. instant vanilla or
   lemon pudding mix
1 lb. strawberries, hulled and
   quartered

1 ripe banana, sliced
1/2 pt. blueberries
1 bunch seedless grapes
Optional: 1 to 2 T. sugar

In a large bowl, combine peaches and pineapple along with the juices from both cans. Sprinkle with dry pudding mix; stir well until dissolved. Stir in remaining fruit and sugar, if desired. Cover and chill before serving. Makes 12 servings.

Cinnamon Applesauce Muffins

Alicia Soncksen
Lincoln, NE

My family begs for more of these delicious spice muffins every time! I tweaked a recipe into a little healthier version. Now I'm happy to hand out seconds!

1/2 c. margarine
2/3 c. brown sugar, packed
2 eggs
2 t. baking powder
1/2 t. baking soda
1 t. cinnamon

1 t. allspice
1 c. light cinnamon applesauce,
   divided
1-1/2 c. all-purpose flour,
   divided

Line a muffin pan with paper liners; spray with non-stick vegetable spray and set aside. In a large bowl, blend margarine and sugar. Add eggs and beat until smooth; blend in baking powder, baking soda and spices. Add 1/2 cup applesauce and one cup flour; stir until blended. Add remaining applesauce and flour; mix well. Fill muffin cups 2/3 full of batter. Bake at 350 degrees for 20 to 24 minutes. Makes one dozen.

Baked Veggies & Bacon

Charlene McCain
Bakersfield, CA

My family requests this delicious side dish whenever we get together. It's wonderful for barbecues and quick dinners, too. Using a microwave cuts down on cooking time, but if you prefer, place all ingredients in a casserole dish and bake at 350 degrees for an hour, or until veggies are tender.

6 to 8 redskin potatoes, cubed
6 carrots, peeled and sliced
2 stalks celery, chopped
1 yellow onion, chopped
1 c. water

salt and pepper to taste
1/4 c. butter, diced
4 slices bacon, crisply cooked
    and crumbled

Combine vegetables in a large microwave-safe dish; add water. Cover dish with plastic wrap. Microwave for 20 minutes, or until vegetables are tender. Drain water; transfer vegetables to an ungreased 3-quart casserole dish. Season with salt and pepper; dot with butter. Top with bacon. Bake, uncovered, at 400 degrees for 15 minutes, or until potatoes begin to turn golden. Do not overbake. Makes 8 servings.

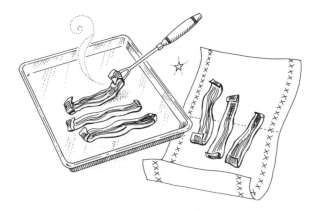

Need just a few slices of bacon for a recipe? Bake it...no muss, no fuss. Arrange bacon slices on a baking sheet. Bake at 350 degrees for 15 to 20 minutes, until it's as crisp as you like. Drain well on paper towels.

Cabin Potatoes

Jamie Guimaraes
Pittsburgh, PA

Every fall, our family travels to Canaan Valley, West Virginia for a week's stay at a cabin we rent. These twice-baked potatoes are the #1 food we have to make there! Friends love them too. They are always requested when we ask what they would like for dinner.

6 T. butter, softened and divided
6 baking potatoes
salt and pepper to taste
1 c. milk
1/2 c. cream cheese, softened
1/2 c. ricotta cheese
8-oz. pkg. bacon bits, divided

3 green onions, chopped
  and divided
1 t. garlic powder
pepper to taste
Optional: shredded Cheddar
  cheese

Use one tablespoon butter to coat potatoes; lightly sprinkle with salt and pepper. Place on a baking sheet; bake at 350 degrees for 1-1/2 hours. Cut potatoes in half lengthwise and scoop out potato pulp, creating shells about 1/4-inch thick. Return potato shells to baking sheet; set aside. In a bowl, add milk to potato pulp. Beat with an electric mixer on low speed until fairly smooth. Add cheeses, remaining butter, half of bacon bits, half of green onions, garlic powder and pepper. Mix well until blended. Spoon mixture back into potato shells, forming mounds. Top potatoes evenly with remaining bacon bits and onions. Sprinkle with Cheddar cheese, if desired. Bake at 350 degrees for about 15 minutes, until heated through and golden on top. Makes 6 servings.

Bring out Mom's vintage Thanksgiving china early to get into the mood for fall. Use the bowls for soup suppers, the teacups for dessert get-togethers and even layer sandwich fixin's on the turkey platter!

Skillet Zucchini

Diana Chaney
Olathe, KS

This veggie dish is a favorite of ours for cooler weather, since the ingredients are readily available year 'round in groceries.

1 T. butter	1 to 2 roma tomatoes, chopped
1 T. olive oil	1 t. dried thyme
3 to 4 zucchini, cubed	salt and pepper to taste
1 onion, chopped	

Add butter and olive oil to a skillet over medium heat. Add zucchini and onion. Cook until zucchini is slightly tender and onion begins to turn translucent, about 5 to 7 minutes. Add tomatoes and seasonings; warm through. Makes 4 servings.

For a quick & easy table runner, choose cotton fabric printed with autumn leaves, Indian corn and pumpkins in bright harvest colors. Simply pink the edges...it will dress up the dinner table all season long.

Baked Refried Beans

Krista Marshall
Fort Wayne, IN

I love making Mexican food at home that tastes like it came from our favorite restaurant...that's just what this is. If you like a little heat, get the spicy variety of refried beans. Make some tacos and dinner is served. Or serve as a dip with chips at your next party.

2 T. butter, sliced
1/4 c. white onion, finely
   chopped
3 cloves garlic, minced
16-oz. can refried beans

1/2 c. cream cheese, softened
1/2 c. shredded Colby Jack
   cheese
Garnish: chopped green onions

Melt butter in a saucepan over medium heat. Sauté onion and garlic until translucent, about 5 to 7 minutes. Add beans; stir well to combine and cook until heated through. Remove from heat. Add cream cheese and stir until melted. Spread mixture in a lightly greased 9" pie plate. Top with shredded cheese. Bake at 350 degrees for 20 minutes, or until hot and bubbly. Garnish with green onions. Makes 4 to 6 servings.

Carve an extra Jack-o'-Lantern or two and deliver to
elderly neighbors so they can enjoy some Halloween fun...
what a neighborly gesture!

Ms. Billie's Old Settlers Baked Beans

Michelle Greeley
Hayes, VA

This recipe was given to me by a very special lady in Idaho.
These are the very best baked beans I have ever eaten!

1 lb. ground beef
1/2 c. onion, chopped
16-oz. can kidney beans
16-oz. can butter beans
16-oz. can pork & beans
2/3 c. brown sugar, packed
1/2 c. catsup

1/4 c. molasses
1/2 c. barbecue sauce
2 T. mustard
1/4 t. chili powder
3 slices bacon, crisply cooked
   and crumbled

Brown beef in a skillet over medium heat. Add onion and cook until tender; drain. Add undrained beans and remaining ingredients except bacon; stir well. Pour into a greased 3-quart casserole dish. Top with bacon. Bake, uncovered, at 350 degrees for one hour. Makes 8 servings.

Everybody loves a tailgating party...and a small-town college rivalry can be just as much fun as a Big Ten game. Load up a pickup truck with tasty finger foods, sandwich fixin's and a big washtub full of bottled drinks on ice. It's all about food and fun!

Cranberry Relish

Mary Ball
Hamilton, MT

I came up with this recipe since my husband didn't like the canned kind. He loves this stuff! He will eat half of it before I can get the turkey on the table. If there's any left, it's even better the next day.

2 navel oranges
12-oz. pkg. fresh cranberries
1 c. sugar
1/2 t. cinnamon

1/8 t. nutmeg
2 Granny Smith apples, cored
and diced
1 c. chopped walnuts

Grate the zest from one orange. Squeeze the juice from both; add enough water to equal a cup, if needed. In a saucepan, combine juice, zest, cranberries and sugar. Cook over medium-high heat until cranberries start to pop. Use a potato masher to mash most of the cranberries. Add spices; continue cooking and stirring until thickened. Stir in apples and walnuts. Remove from heat; cool before serving. Makes 6 to 8 servings.

Maple-Cinnamon Fried Apples

Dawn Raskiewicz
Alliance, NE

We love fried apples and I thought I would give them a little twist for fall. I do not add any sugar to the apples because I find their natural sweetness is enough.

1/4 c. butter, sliced
4 c. Braeburn or Fuji apples,
cored and sliced

2 t. maple flavored extract
cinnamon to taste

Melt butter in a skillet over medium heat. Add apples; sprinkle with extract and cinnamon. Cook for about 20 minutes, turning several times, until tender and golden. More cinnamon may be added, if desired. Serve warm. Makes 3 to 4 servings.

Apricot-Pine Nut Stuffing

Janis Parr
Ontario, Canada

This is for stuffing lovers! It's both traditional and different, and oh-so-good!

6-oz. pkg. dried apricots, finely chopped
1/2 c. orange juice
1/4 c. butter, sliced
1 onion, chopped
1/2 c. celery, chopped
1 Granny Smith apple, peeled, cored and chopped
1/2 c. pine nuts or chopped almonds
6 c. soft bread cubes
1 t. dried sage
1 t. salt
pepper to taste
Optional: 1 egg, beaten

In a small saucepan over low heat, simmer apricots with orange juice for 5 minutes, or until fruit is soft. Meanwhile, melt butter in a skillet over medium heat. Add onion and celery; cook until soft. Combine apricot and onion mixtures in a large bowl. Add remaining ingredients, adding egg if a moister stuffing is desired; toss very well. Spoon mixture into a greased 3-quart casserole dish. Cover and bake at 325 degrees for one hour. Serve hot. Makes 8 to 10 servings.

One of my favorite memories was in 4th grade when I entered a pumpkin carving contest at school. Dad found the most unique, misshapen pumpkin with great big cheeks. He helped me carve the face after I drew it. The pumpkin wouldn't stay upright, so he cut a bowtie out of wood and attached it to support the chin. I colored the bowtie green. I won the contest for my grade and got my picture in the newspaper. Dad and I were so proud of our cheeky pumpkin! That's a day I will never forget...the photo still gives me a chuckle. Sometimes I wish I could go back, knowing now how precious those moments with my family really were.

-Diane Goertzen, White Bear Lake, MN

Farmstand Filled Acorn Squash *Jackie Smulski*
Lyons, IL

When the season is winding down for farmers' markets, don't hang up your basket just yet! There are freshly picked apples and squash. This delicious dish is wonderful for a chilly autumn day.

1 to 2 acorn squash, quartered and seeds removed	2 t. butter, melted
	2 t. brown sugar, packed
1 Golden Delicious apple, peeled, cored and sliced	1/4 t. cinnamon
	1/4 t. nutmeg
1/4 c. golden raisins	1/8 t. ground cloves

Halve squash and remove seeds; cut squash into quarters. Place squash quarters cut-side down in a buttered one-quart casserole dish. Cover and bake at 350 degrees for 30 minutes. Meanwhile, combine apples, raisins, butter, brown sugar and spices in a bowl; mix well. Turn squash quarters cut-side up; top with apple mixture. Cover and bake 30 minutes longer, or until tender. Makes 4 servings.

Grab a girlfriend and head for a late-autumn farmers' market! You'll find colorful fall produce, homemade apple butter and maybe even fresh-baked cookies to share.

Grandma's Special Cornbread Bake

Martha Stapler
Sanford, FL

While making my usual cornbread, I decided to use up some items in the fridge. The result was really delicious!

2 bunches broccoli, cut into
    bite-size flowerets
2 8-1/2 oz. pkgs. corn
    muffin mix
2 onions, chopped
1 small jalapeño pepper,
    seeded and minced

salt and pepper to taste
6 eggs, beaten
1-1/2 c. milk
8-oz. pkg. shredded sharp
    Cheddar cheese

Bring a large saucepan of water to a boil over high heat. Add broccoli; cook for 3 to 4 minutes, until crisp-tender. Drain; transfer broccoli to a large bowl. Add dry corn muffin mix, onions and jalapeño pepper; season with salt and pepper. In a separate bowl, whisk together eggs and milk. Add to broccoli mixture; stir well. Pour batter into a greased deep 11"x9" baking pan. Bake, uncovered, at 350 degrees for 40 minutes. Top with cheese; bake an additional 5 minutes, or until cheese is melted. Let stand for 20 minutes before slicing. Makes 10 to 12 servings.

Add an extra can or two of soup, veggies or tuna to the grocery cart every week, then put aside these extras at home. Before you know it, you'll have a generous selection of canned goods for fall food drives.

Kristin's Sweet & Tangy Green Beans

Lisa Kastning
Marysville, WA

My friend Kristin shared this recipe with me over 20 years ago, and it's still one of my favorite ways to eat green beans. I've never tasted anything like them...hope you enjoy them too!

2 15-oz. cans French-cut
   green beans
1 c. sliced mushrooms
1/2 c. onion, diced
2 T. butter, sliced
8-oz. can water chestnuts,
   drained and chopped

1 c. sour cream
1 t. sugar
1 t. salt
1 t. vinegar

Add green beans with liquid to a saucepan. Heat over low heat until warmed through; drain. Meanwhile, in a skillet over medium heat, sauté mushrooms and onion in butter until tender, 5 to 7 minutes. Stir in water chestnuts. In a bowl, whisk together sour cream and remaining ingredients; add to mushroom mixture and warm through. Pour over warmed green beans. Stir gently and serve. Serves 6.

At sit-down dinners, encourage table talk among guests who don't know each other well. Just write each person's name on both sides of the placecard so other guests can see it.

Pineapple-Glazed Sweet Potatoes

Nancy Wise
Little Rock, AR

With Thanksgiving coming up, I was looking for a different way to serve sweet potatoes. My friend Andrea shared this recipe with me...it was a hit with my family!

1-1/2 lbs. sweet potatoes, peeled and cut into cubes
1/3 c. sweetened dried cranberries
1/4 c. brown sugar, packed

3 T. butter, melted
1 t. cinnamon
20-oz. can pineapple chunks in juice, drained and 1/4 c. juice reserved

In a greased 2-quart casserole dish, combine sweet potatoes, cranberries, brown sugar, melted butter, cinnamon and reserved pineapple juice. Stir gently. Cover and bake at 375 degrees for 30 to 40 minutes, until sweet potatoes are tender. Stir in pineapple chunks. Return to oven, uncovered, for about 5 minutes, until heated through. Makes 6 servings.

A quick fall craft for kids...hot glue large acorn caps onto round magnets for whimsical fridge magnets.

Mimi's Harvard Beets

Carol Bower
Maumee, OH

My Grandmother Mimi would make this often for Sunday dinner. The menu rarely changed. The tangy beets were served alongside rump roast, mashed potatoes & gravy, creamed cauliflower, dinner rolls and homemade lemon meringue pie! I still fondly recall the delicious smells as I walked into her home.

1/3 c. boiling water	1/2 t. salt
1/3 c. cider vinegar	2 15-oz. cans diced or sliced
1/2 c. sugar	beets, drained
1 T. cornstarch	Optional: 2 T. butter

In a saucepan, combine all ingredients except beets and butter. Cook over medium heat, stirring often, until cornstarch dissolves and a clear sauce forms. Reduce heat to low. If sliced beets are used, dice them. Add beets to saucepan. Stir well and simmer until beets are heated through. If desired, stir in butter. Serve warm. Makes 8 servings.

Take time to share family stories and traditions with
your kids over the dinner table. A cherished family recipe
can be a super conversation starter.

Mary's Cornbread Dressing

Pam McDaniel
Sunnyvale, TX

This was my sweet mother-in-law Mary's recipe. When I think of this dish I can almost smell it...she was hands-down the best and most patient cook I have ever known! She always made this for our Thanksgiving and Christmas meals. She had a garden and always made everything from scratch. It's the best dressing I have ever had. I still have the recipe written in her handwriting.

2 8-1/2 oz. pkgs. corn
   muffin mix
16-oz. tube refrigerated
   buttermilk biscuits
1/2 c. butter, sliced
2 onions, chopped
2 c. celery, chopped

4 eggs
1 T. dried sage
salt and pepper to taste
10-3/4 oz. can cream of
   chicken soup
3 to 4 c. chicken broth

The day before, prepare corn muffin mix according to package directions; bake in a 13"x9" baking pan. Bake biscuits according to package directions. Cool; set aside. The next day, melt butter in a skillet over medium heat. Add onions and celery; cook until tender. Remove from heat; do not drain. In a very large bowl, beat eggs with sage, salt and pepper. Crumble cornbread and biscuits; add to egg mixture and stir well. Add onion mixture, soup and enough broth to moisten; mix well. Transfer dressing mixture to a greased 13"x9" baking pan. Cover and bake at 350 degrees for 45 to 50 minutes. For a crisper top, uncover for the last 15 minutes. Makes 10 to 12 servings.

Grandma never tossed out day-old bread and neither should you! It keeps its texture better than very fresh bread...it's thrifty too. Cut it into cubes, pack into freezer bags and freeze for making stuffing cubes, casserole toppings and herbed salad croutons.

Edamame Succotash

Robin Hill
Rochester, NY

Edamame beans are a fun update for a dish that goes back to the Pilgrims. Feel free to substitute baby lima beans.

1 to 2 slices bacon	1 red pepper, diced
1 T. butter	3 roma tomatoes, diced
1 sweet onion, diced	2 T. red wine vinegar
2 c. frozen corn, thawed	1/2 t. sugar
2 c. frozen shelled edamame,	salt and pepper to taste
thawed	2 T. fresh basil, chopped

In a skillet over medium heat, cook bacon until crisp. Set aside bacon; reserve drippings in pan. Turn heat to medium-high. Add butter and onion to reserved drippings. Cook for 3 minutes, stirring occasionally. Add corn; cook for 3 minutes. Add edamame and red pepper; cook for 3 minutes. Stir in remaining ingredients except basil; cook and stir for 30 seconds. Garnish with crumbled bacon and basil. Makes 6 to 8 servings.

Steakhouse Broccoli Spears

Michelle Powell
Valley, AL

This savory sauce keeps for weeks in the fridge. Serve over steamed broccoli for a quick supper side.

1 bunch broccoli, cut into	1 T. prepared horseradish
serving-size stalks	1 T. onion, grated
salt to taste	1/4 t. salt
1/4 c. butter, melted	1/4 t. dry mustard
1/4 c. mayonnaise	1/8 t. cayenne pepper

Peel broccoli stalks with a vegetable peeler, if desired. Add to a saucepan of boiling salted water over medium-high heat. Cook until crisp-tender, about 8 minutes. Meanwhile, combine remaining ingredients in a bowl; blend well. Drain broccoli; season lightly with salt. Serve topped with a spoonful of sauce. Makes 6 servings.

Crispy Smashed Potatoes

Tracy Burdyshaw
Perry, OH

When my kids are all home for the holidays, I need an easy, filling dish that is also delicious and nutritious. Think 6'5" basketball and football players! This is their favorite potato dish, without the fat of fries or loaded baked potatoes, nor the time mashed potatoes demand.

3 lbs. new redskin potatoes
1/2 c. olive oil, divided

garlic powder, dried basil, salt and pepper to taste

Cover whole potatoes with water in a saucepan. Cook over medium-high heat until just fork-tender, 10 to 15 minutes; drain. Line a baking sheet with foil. Brush foil lightly with some oil. Transfer potatoes to baking sheet and press down halfway to flatten, using the bottom of a drinking glass. Brush potatoes with remaining oil. Season to taste as desired. Bake, uncovered, at 450 degrees for 20 to 25 minutes, until potatoes are crisp and golden. Makes 4 to 6 servings.

Tie up bunches of herbs to dry and hang them in your kitchen. They'll add the freshest taste to those simmering soups & stews and wonderful comfort foods you'll be making all harvest season long.

Creamy Party Potatoes

*Diana Krol
Nickerson, KS*

These are the only mashed potatoes I make for our family! I was introduced to this recipe at our church's dinner. The ladies make the potatoes ahead of time, then serve them from slow cookers with turkey and brisket meals. With or without gravy, they're delicious!

5 lbs. russet potatoes, peeled and cubed	2 T. butter, sliced
3/4 c. cream cheese, softened	2 t. onion salt
1 c. sour cream	1 t. salt
	1/4 t. pepper

Cover potatoes with water in a saucepan over medium-high heat. Bring to a boil; cook until fork-tender. Drain and transfer to a bowl; mash until smooth. Add remaining ingredients; beat until light and fluffy. Serve immediately, or transfer to a slow cooker and hold on low setting until ready to serve. Potatoes may also be cooled, covered and refrigerated for 3 to 4 days; reheat at serving time. Makes 8 to 10 servings.

Whimsical candlesticks...use a paring knife to carve a hole in the center of mini pumpkins. Make it just big enough so that a taper will sit snugly. Set each pumpkin on top of a candlestick so it will be level. Clever!

Honey-Kissed Carrots

Ellen Folkman
Crystal Beach, FL

This is a favorite recipe in my home. I often cook the carrots in a steamer, then transfer to a bowl and add the remaining ingredients. It's easy to double for a larger crowd.

1 lb. carrots, peeled and sliced
   1/2-inch thick
1/4 c. water

1/3 c. golden raisins
1/3 c. honey
2 T. butter

In a saucepan over medium heat, combine carrots and water. Cover and simmer 15 minutes, or until tender. Add remaining ingredients. Simmer, uncovered, until carrots are glazed, about 10 minutes, stirring occasionally. Makes 4 servings.

Brown Sugar Acorn Squash

Deanna Adams
Garland, TX

My dad always had a large garden in the summer, and I have wonderful memories of meals made with fresh vegetables in season. As fall came, most of this bounty was gone, but then came the acorn squash! This is my mom's simple way of preparing them. Honey or maple syrup could be used instead of brown sugar.

2 acorn squash, halved or
   quartered and seeds removed

4 T. butter
8 T. brown sugar, packed

Slice a bit off the bottom of squash pieces so that they will lie flat. Place squash in a 13"x9" glass baking pan. Fill each squash piece with one tablespoon butter and 2 tablespoons brown sugar. Cover and bake at 350 degrees for 30 to 40 minutes, until tender. Serves 2 to 4.

Make acorn squash easier to cut! Pierce the skin of the uncut squash several times with a knife point, then pop it in the microwave and cook on high for 2 minutes.

Slow-Cooked Roasted Root Vegetables

Elizabeth Blackstone
Racine, WI

This recipe is so handy when other dishes will be baking in the oven. Fill up the crock with any of your favorite root veggies! Sweet potatoes, parsnips, sweet onions and celery root are delicious too.

4 russet potatoes, cut into
   1-1/2 inch cubes
1 lb. baby carrots
1 onion, chopped
2 cloves garlic, minced

2 T. water
3 T. olive oil
1/4 t. salt
1/8 t. pepper

Combine vegetables in a 4-quart slow cooker. Sprinkle with remaining ingredients; stir to combine. Cover and cook on low setting for 7 to 9 hours, until vegetables fork-tender. Makes 6 to 8 servings.

I have many fond memories of Halloween in our childhood home. My mom was a cake designer and very crafty. She made Halloween pizza for us before we went out. Once she got us out the door with Dad for trick-or-treating, she began her surprises for us. When we came home, Mom would have the house decorated and goodies on a beautifully decorated table. Mom was famous for her witch cakes and would make mini versions for us kids. Hot apple cider and other scents of the season bring me home to those favorite memories that I have recreated for my children and now for my grandchildren.

-Carole Sylvia, Nashua, NH

Crunchy Veggie Bake

Lori Ritchey
Denver, PA

This casserole with its crunchy topping is always a hit with kids and adults...it's a sneaky way to get them to eat their veggies! I make this for company as well as for our church fellowship meals.

2 10-3/4 oz. cans cream of
    mushroom soup
1 c. mayonnaise
1 T. garlic powder
1/4 t. pepper
8-oz. pkg. shredded Cheddar
    cheese

3 16-oz. pkgs. frozen broccoli,
    carrot and cauliflower blend,
    thawed
6-oz. can French fried onions

In a bowl, combine soup, mayonnaise and seasonings; mix well. Stir in cheese and set aside. Spread vegetables in a greased 13"x9" baking pan. Spoon soup mixture over veggies; toss evenly to coat. Bake, uncovered, at 350 degrees for 35 to 40 minutes. Sprinkle with onions. Bake an additional 5 minutes, or until onions are golden. Makes 10 to 12 servings.

Choose the prettiest leaves to preserve for crafting and decorating. Arrange leaves in a flat pan and cover with a mixture of one part glycerin and 2 parts water. Use a rock to keep the leaves submerged for one week, then remove and blot dry with paper towels...they'll retain their brilliant colors all season long.

Harvest Dinner
Mains

Aunt Pauli's Oktoberfest Supper
Kirsten Pettie
Fargo, ND

This recipe was shared by my Aunt Pauli when my sister was getting married. Our mom made us both a family cookbook as a shower gift.

6 slices bacon
4 potatoes, sliced
1 onion, sliced and separated
   into rings
3 carrots, peeled and sliced

1 bunch broccoli, cut into
   flowerets
1 lb. smoked pork sausage or
   Kielbasa, cut into 1-inch
   pieces

Cook bacon in a large skillet over medium heat until crisp. Remove bacon to paper towels; reserve drippings in skillet. Sauté vegetables in reserved drippings until tender. Top with sausage. Cover and cook for 10 to 12 minutes, until sausage is browned. Garnish with crumbled bacon. Makes 6 servings.

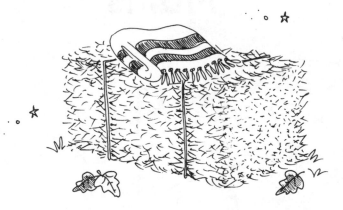

Short on chairs for a backyard gathering? Arrange hay bales for super easy, country-style seating.

Debbie's Skillet Pasta

Debbie Swank
Wauseon, OH

This is such an easy recipe and very tasty. My family loves it. Just add a tossed salad and garlic cheese bread for a hearty meal.

3 c. penne pasta, uncooked
1 lb. ground beef
garlic powder, onion powder and
    pepper to taste

28-oz. jar pasta sauce
8-oz. pkg. shredded mozzarella
    cheese, divided
1/2 c. grated Parmesan cheese

Cook pasta according to package directions; drain. Meanwhile, brown beef in a large skillet over medium heat; drain and add seasonings. Add cooked pasta, pasta sauce and one cup cheese to skillet; stir until combined. Sprinkle with Parmesan cheese and remaining mozzarella cheese. Cover and simmer until cheese is melted. Makes 6 servings.

Pesto Garlic Bread

Leah McGowen
Reno, NV

This recipe was first created by my Aunt Mary Ellen. Years later, I revamped it and made it my own. This bread is always a huge hit and complements just about any main dish or soup.

1 c. grated Parmesan cheese
1 c. mayonnaise
1 c. butter, softened
1/4 c. pesto sauce
2 to 3 T. garlic powder

1 loaf Italian bread, halved
    lengthwise
Italian seasoning, dried oregano
    and paprika to taste

In a bowl, combine all ingredients except bread and seasonings; stir to a smooth consistency. Spread mixture on cut sides of bread; sprinkle with seasonings. Set oven broiler to low; place bread on broiler pan. Broil 12 inches below broiler for 2 to 3 minutes, or until bubbly and edges are lightly golden. Cool; cut into thick slices and serve. Makes 6 to 8 servings.

Loaded Potato & Chicken Casserole

Susie Backus
Delaware, OH

This casserole is the ultimate comfort food! Everyone in my family cleans their plate when I serve this.

2-1/2 lbs. boneless, skinless chicken breasts, cubed
3 lbs. new redskin potatoes, cut into bite-size pieces
2/3 c. extra-virgin olive oil
2 t. garlic powder
1 t. salt
1 t. pepper

2 to 3 c. shredded sharp Cheddar cheese
1 lb. bacon, crisply cooked and crumbled
3 green onions, sliced
Garnish: sour cream or ranch salad dressing

Place chicken and potatoes in a large bowl. In a separate bowl, mix oil and seasonings. Pour oil mixture over chicken mixture; toss until coated. Transfer to a 13"x9" baking pan sprayed with non-stick vegetable spray. Bake, uncovered, at 400 degrees for 60 to 70 minutes, stirring every 20 minutes. Remove from oven; top with cheese, crumbled bacon and green onions. Bake another 5 to 10 minutes, until cheese is melted. Garnish with sour cream or ranch dressing. Makes 10 servings.

Make a cornhusk wreath! Remove the husks from dried ears of corn and fold them in half. Wrap ends with thin wire and insert the wires into a straw wreath, covering all sides. Add dried yarrow, bittersweet and wheat for a wonderful welcome-to-fall decoration.

Pork & Cabbage Dinner

Marilyn Morel
Keene, NH

Nothing says fall and comfort like this dinner. Welcome your family with the tantalizing cooking aromas, then be prepared for lots of praise!

1 T. butter	1/2 c. apple juice
2 T. olive oil	1-1/2 t. caraway seed
4 boneless pork chops	3/4 t. dried thyme
salt and pepper to taste	1/2 lb. Kielbasa sausage,
1/2 head cabbage, thinly sliced	sliced 1/4-inch thick
2 carrots, peeled and shredded	2 T. cider vinegar

Melt butter with oil in a large heavy skillet over medium heat. Season pork chops with salt and pepper; add to skillet and cook on both sides until golden. Remove pork chops from skillet; reserve drippings in skillet. Add cabbage, carrots, apple juice, caraway seed and thyme. Stir to combine. Cover and cook for 8 to 10 minutes over medium heat, stirring occasionally, until cabbage is tender. Add Kielbasa and vinegar; return pork chops to skillet. Cover and cook over medium-low heat for 5 minutes, stirring occasionally, until pork is no longer pink. Remove from heat; let stand for 5 minutes before serving. Makes 4 servings.

Host a neighborhood spruce-up! Everyone can help trim bushes and pull bloomed-out annuals...even kids can rake leaves. End with a simple supper for all.

Greek Chicken & Spaghetti

Victoria Mitchel
Gettysburg, PA

My dear friend Christy shared this recipe with me and it was a hit with everyone in my family. Over the years, I've tweaked it a little here & there to make it just perfect for our taste. It's sure to please even the pickiest of eaters. We like to serve ours with crusty bread and a side salad. Leftovers taste good hot or cold.

16-oz. pkg. spaghetti, uncooked
1 T. olive oil
1 lb. boneless, skinless chicken breast, cut into bite-size cubes
1 green pepper, diced
1/2 c. red onion, diced
1/2 c. sliced black olives
1/2 to 3/4 c. crumbled feta cheese
4 plum tomatoes, chopped
1 c. Greek salad dressing

Cook pasta according to package directions; drain and return to pan. Meanwhile, heat oil in a large skillet over medium heat. Add chicken; cook until golden on all sides. Add green pepper, onion and olives; cook until vegetables have softened. Add chicken mixture and remaining ingredients to cooked spaghetti. Toss to mix together well; warm through over low heat. Makes 4 to 6 servings.

Start a new Thanksgiving tradition. Decorate a blank book
and invite everyone to write what they're thankful for.
The tradition will become even more meaningful
as it's continued, year after year.

Chicken Taco Pie

Emily Martin
Ontario, Canada

Even my younger kids can help me mix up this tasty dinner pie!
They love to see how the pie makes its own crust as it
bakes in the oven. A one-dish dinner in a jiffy!

2 c. cooked chicken, cubed
1/2 c. onion, chopped
2 T. taco seasoning mix
1 c. biscuit baking mix
1 c. milk
2 eggs, beaten

1 c. shredded Mexican-blend
  cheese
Garnish: shredded lettuce, diced
  tomatoes, sliced black olives,
  sour cream

Combine chicken, onion and taco seasoning in a greased 9" glass pie plate. Mix gently and set aside. In a bowl, combine biscuit mix, milk and eggs; stir with a fork until blended. Pour batter over chicken mixture in pie plate. Bake at 400 degrees for 30 to 35 minutes, until a knife tip inserted in the center tests clean. Sprinkle with cheese. Return to oven for one to 2 minutes longer, until cheese is melted. Cut into wedges. Garnish each wedge. Makes 8 servings.

One of the best fall memories I've had occurred several years ago. We went to West Virginia to see our son and grandkids and visited to a nice farm outside of town. It was a rather hot day for October but we went on a ride all around the farm with the girls. They had a great time seeing the sights, including the buffalo! We meandered through the corn fields and into the pumpkin fields where we walked around looking for the "just right" pumpkin for each granddaughter. The looks on the children's faces as they picked their very own pumpkins were priceless! Photos were taken, but the pictures in my heart will last much longer.

-Maybelline Rice, Jacksonville, FL

Speedy Tamale Pie

Kelly Cook
Dunedin, FL

Ready-made tamales make this pie oh-so quick. This makes enough for a crowd, so it's perfect to take to a church supper or family reunion.

2 15-oz. cans beef tamales, divided
15-oz. can chili, divided
9-1/4 oz. pkg. corn chips, divided

1 onion, minced and divided
2 c. shredded Cheddar cheese, divided

Chop one can of tamales; set aside. Spread one cup chili in the bottom of a greased 2-quart casserole dish; layer half the corn chips, half the onion and chopped tamales on top. Sprinkle with half the cheese; repeat layers, ending with whole tamales topped with cheese. Cover and bake at 350 degrees for one hour. Let stand 10 minutes before serving. Makes 12 servings.

Let the kids invite a special friend or two home for dinner. Keep it simple with a hearty casserole and a relish tray of crunchy veggies & dip. A great way to get to know your children's new school pals!

Harvest Dinner

Mains

Cheesy Mexican Calzones

Lori Ritchey
Denver, PA

Bored with tacos? You'll love this quick new way to have Mexican!

1 lb. ground beef
4-oz. can diced green chiles
1/4 c. water
1-1/4 oz. pkg. taco seasoning
   mix
15-oz. pkg. refrigerated pie
   crusts, room temperature

8-oz. pkg. shredded Mexican-
   blend cheese, divided
Garnish: shredded lettuce,
   diced tomatoes, sliced green
   onions, salsa, sour cream

Brown beef in a large skillet over medium heat; drain. Add chiles, water and taco seasoning; stir well. Unfold pie crusts on a cutting board. Cut each crust in half, making 4 half-circles. Spoon 1/2 cup beef mixture onto half of each circle; top with 1/4 cup cheese. Moisten edges of crusts with a little water. Fold crusts over filling; crimp edges with a fork. Place calzones on an ungreased baking sheet. Bake at 425 degrees for 10 minutes. Remove from oven; sprinkle with remaining cheese. Bake 5 to 8 minutes more, until cheese melts. Garnish with desired toppings. Makes 4 servings.

Clever placecards...childhood photos at each place setting.
Not only do they bring sweet memories, but it's fun
to guess who's who!

French Bread Pizza

Penny Sherman
Ava, MO

At our house, we have family fun night every Friday. My older son helps me put together this easy, cheesy pizza while the younger kids are helping their dad choose a board game or a favorite movie. It makes for a very cozy evening together and a lot of memories.

1-lb. loaf French bread,
   halved lengthwise
1 lb. lean ground beef
1 onion, chopped
15-oz. can tomato sauce

2 t. Italian seasoning
8-oz. pkg. shredded
   mozzarella cheese
3-oz. pkg. sliced pepperoni

Place bread on an aluminum foil-covered baking sheet. In a large skillet over medium heat, brown beef with onion; drain. Stir in tomato sauce and seasoning. Simmer for 5 minutes, stirring occasionally. Spread beef mixture onto bread slices; top with cheese and desired amount of pepperoni. Bake at 400 degrees for 10 to 12 minutes, until cheese is melted. Slice bread into serving-size pieces. Serves 4.

As the weather cools, every sofa should have an inviting throw folded over the back for snuggling! Why not pull out that afghan Great-Aunt Sophie crocheted years ago, or a treasured baby quilt that's been outgrown?

Chili Cheese Dog Casserole

Marie King
Independence, MO

I created this recipe because I wanted chili dogs without all the messiness of a bun. We like to eat it in a bowl with tortilla chips for dipping, almost like nachos!

8 hot dogs, sliced
1 onion, diced
1 clove garlic, diced
3 to 4 c. favorite homemade
    or canned chili
11-oz. can corn, drained
1/2 c. shredded Cheddar cheese
32-oz. pkg. frozen potato puffs,
    divided
tortilla or corn chips

In a lightly greased large skillet over medium heat, combine hot dogs, onion and garlic. Cook until lightly golden, about 10 to 15 minutes. Add chili and corn; stir well. Spoon mixture into an ungreased 13"x9" glass baking pan. Top evenly with cheese. Arrange enough frozen potato puffs to just cover top without touching each other. Return any remaining potato puffs to the freezer for another recipe. Cover with aluminum foil. Bake at 350 degrees for 45 to 50 minutes, until potato puffs cook and sink down into chili mixture. Remove from oven; let cool for 10 to 15 minutes. Serve in bowls, with chips for dipping. Makes 8 to 10 servings.

Host a backyard bonfire weenie roast in the fall when the weather turns cool and crisp. Serve up hearty baked beans and simmering spiced cider...for dessert, toast marshmallows for s'mores. Sure to warm hearts as well as hands!

Dinner in a Pumpkin

Ellie Brandel
Clackamas, OR

This delicious, hearty meal is a great autumn recipe
for families...such fun to serve at the table!

1 medium pumpkin
1-1/2 c. celery, chopped
1 c. onion, chopped
4-oz. can sliced mushrooms,
    drained
1 T. butter

1 lb. ground beef
10-3/4 oz. can cream of
    chicken soup
4 c. cooked rice
1/2 c. soy sauce
2 T. brown sugar, packed

Cut the top off pumpkin; remove seeds and clean out the inside well.
Set aside pumpkin and pumpkin top. In a skillet over medium heat,
sauté celery, onion and mushrooms in butter. Remove celery mixture
to a large bowl; set aside. Brown beef in the same skillet; drain well.
Combine beef and remaining ingredients with celery mixture; stir well.
Spoon mixture into pumpkin; replace top. Set pumpkin on a baking
sheet. Bake at 350 degrees for one hour. To serve, scoop out some of
the inside of the pumpkin along with filling. Makes 6 to 8 servings.

Roasted pumpkin seeds are delicious for snacking!
Rinse 2 cups of seeds; dry on paper towels. Toss with
one tablespoon of oil and place on an ungreased baking sheet.
Bake at 350 degrees for 20 minutes; stir every 5 minutes.
Remove from oven and sprinkle with salt.

Harvest Fest Pork Chops

Judy Lange
Imperial, PA

Fall is in the air when I prepare these delicious pork chops.
I serve baked apples on the side...yummy!

1 T. oil or bacon drippings
4 boneless pork chops
16-oz. jar sauerkraut
8-oz. jar applesauce

1/4 c. onion, chopped
2 T. brown sugar, packed
salt and pepper to taste

Heat drippings or oil in a skillet over medium heat. Brown pork chops on both sides; drain. Combine sauerkraut with liquid, applesauce, onion and brown sugar in a bowl; spoon over pork chops. Season with salt and pepper. Reduce heat to medium-low. Cover and simmer until pork chops are done, about 45 minutes. Makes 4 servings.

I grew up on the south side of Chicago, and needless to say,
I didn't have much experience with a real wheat harvest.
However, when I met and married my husband, who grew up
on a farm in Kansas, I quickly realized what an important time
of the year harvest was! I will never forget the first few harvests
that I was a part of. I was amazed by the skill, patience and grace
that my new mother in-law displayed as she prepared hearty
meals for the harvest "crew" of her husband, children and
grandchildren. What most impressed me was that, no matter
what time the crew planned to eat, that's when the hot food
would be on the table. She knew that time was of the essence.
She played a huge role in the efficiency and success of harvest...
and this city girl learned a lot by watching her!

-Laurie Regehr, Halstead, KS

Simple Dirty Rice for a Crowd
Michelle Powell
Valley, AL

Easiest rice dish ever...delicious every time! Great for big get-togethers and potlucks.

2 lbs. ground pork sausage
1 lb. ground beef
1 c. onion, diced
9 c. water
2 c. long-cooking rice, uncooked
1 c. celery, chopped

3 2-1/4 oz. pkgs. noodle soup
   mix with chicken broth
8-oz. can sliced mushrooms
salt and pepper to taste
8-oz. can sliced water chestnuts,
   drained

Brown sausage and beef with onion in a large skillet over medium heat. Drain; set aside. Meanwhile, add water to a stockpot; bring to a boil over high heat. Stir in rice, celery and soup mixes. Reduce heat to medium-low. Simmer until rice is tender and water is nearly absorbed, stirring occasionally. Add sausage mixture and mushrooms with liquid. Season with salt and pepper. Divide mixture between 2 lightly greased 13"x9" glass baking pans. Top with water chestnuts. Bake, uncovered, at 350 degrees for 25 minutes. Makes 15 servings.

G-hosting a Halloween buffet? Offer a selection of creepy foods and beverages, labeled with table tents in your spookiest handwriting. Do you have a specialty that isn't Halloween-inspired? Just give it a spooky new name!

Steph's Sour Cream Enchiladas

Stephanie D'Esposito
Ravena, NY

My best friend Christy and I enjoy these delicious enchiladas any chance we get. The slow-cooked chicken is juicy and tender. They are definitely as good as you'd get in a restaurant. Delicious!

4 boneless, skinless chicken breasts
1/2 onion, diced
1-1/4 oz. pkg. taco seasoning mix
3 c. chicken broth, divided
1/4 c. butter, sliced
1/4 c. all-purpose flour

1 c. sour cream
4-oz. can chopped green chiles
8 fajita-size flour tortillas
3 c. shredded Mexican-blend cheese, divided
Garnish: chopped lettuce, sliced tomatoes, chopped fresh cilantro, guacamole

Place chicken in a 4-quart slow cooker; set aside. In a bowl, mix onion, taco seasoning and one cup broth; pour over chicken. Cover and cook on low setting for 4 hours, or until very tender. Remove chicken to a plate; shred and set aside. Melt butter in a saucepan over medium-low heat; sprinkle with flour. Cook and stir until bubbly; continue cooking for one minute. Add remaining broth to saucepan. Bring to a boil; cook until thickened, stirring often. Remove from heat; stir in sour cream and chiles. To assemble, top each flour tortilla with 1/4 cup chicken and a sprinkle of cheese. Roll up and place in a lightly greased 13"x9" baking pan, seam-side down. Spoon sour cream mixture over enchiladas; sprinkle with remaining cheese. Bake, uncovered, at 350 degrees for 35 minutes. Serve enchiladas garnished as desired. Makes 4 servings, 2 enchiladas each.

Start your own Halloween dinner tradition! In the morning, put on a favorite slow-cooker dish to simmer. It will be easy for everyone to serve themselves before putting on costumes or in between handing out treats.

Bake & Share BBQ Meatballs

Diana Krol
Nickerson, KS

This is a wonderful recipe to share with friends. Bake a pan for your family and share a second pan with others. Or enjoy now and hide a pan in your freezer for later. The meatballs can easily be made ahead of time and baked as needed.

3 lbs. lean ground beef or turkey
1 c. evaporated milk
2 c. quick-cooking oats, uncooked
2 eggs, beaten

1 onion, chopped
2 t. chili powder
1/2 t. garlic salt
1/2 t. pepper

Combine all ingredients in a large bowl; mix well. Form into 2-inch balls, by hand or using a small scoop. Place meatballs in a single layer in 2 ungreased 13"x9" baking pans. If desired, cover and refrigerate up to one day, or wrap well and freeze. Spoon hot BBQ Sauce over meatballs, thawed if frozen. Cover and bake at 350 degrees for one hour, until bubbly and meatballs are no longer pink in the center. Makes 24 servings.

BBQ Sauce:

2 c. catsup
1-1/2 c. brown sugar, packed
1/2 c. onion, chopped

2 T. smoke-flavored cooking sauce
1/2 t. garlic powder

Combine all ingredients; mix well. Microwave or simmer in a saucepan until heated through and brown sugar is dissolved.

Tasty meatballs are so versatile during the holiday season. Make up a big batch to store in the season, then thaw as needed and serve as meatball sandwiches, spaghetti & meatballs, even party appetizers. Always sure to be a hit!

Easy-Cheesy Stuffed Shells

Anne Alesauskas
Minocqua, WI

*I always make this pasta dish when I have a crowd coming
for dinner. It's super easy and I can make it up ahead of time,
so there's more time to spend with my guests!*

24 jumbo pasta shells, uncooked
1 lb. lean ground beef
26-oz. jar pasta sauce
1/4 c. water
8-oz. pkg. shredded Italian-
  blend cheese, divided

8-oz. container chives & onion
  cream cheese spread
1/2 c. grated Parmesan cheese
1 egg, beaten
Garnish: 1 to 2 T. fresh parsley,
  chopped

Cook pasta shells according to package directions, just until tender;
drain. Meanwhile, brown beef in a skillet over medium heat; drain and
cool slightly. In a large bowl, combine pasta sauce and water. Spread
one cup of sauce mixture in the bottom of an ungreased 13"x9" baking
pan; set aside. In a separate bowl, combine beef, one cup Italian-blend
cheese and remaining ingredients except parsley; mix well. Spoon a
heaping tablespoonful of beef mixture into each shell. Arrange stuffed
shells over sauce in baking pan. Spoon remaining sauce over shells,
covering completely. Cover with aluminum foil. Bake at 350 degrees
for 40 to 45 minutes, until hot and bubbly. Sprinkle with remaining
Italian-blend cheese; bake 10 minutes longer. Sprinkle with parsley.
Makes 8 to 10 servings.

Create a fall centerpiece in a snap! Hot-glue ears of
mini Indian corn around a terra cotta pot and set a vase
of orange or yellow mums in the center.

Spaghetti for a Crowd

Carrie Kelderman
Pella, IA

This is a Kelderman family favorite! This recipe was passed on to me from my mother-in-law Judy, and has been enjoyed since my husband was a little boy. It's a freezer meal...so convenient.

16-oz. pkg. thin spaghetti,
  uncooked
2-1/2 lbs. ground beef
1 T. dried minced onion
1 t. dried oregano

48-oz. jar pasta sauce
1 c. grated Parmesan cheese
16-oz. pkg. shredded Cheddar
  cheese

Cook spaghetti according to package directions; drain and return to pan. Meanwhile, brown beef in a skillet over medium heat; drain. Stir in onion and oregano. To cooked spaghetti, add beef mixture, sauce and Parmesan cheese; mix well. Divide between 2 greased 13"x9" baking pans or 4, 8"x8" baking pans. Top with Cheddar cheese. Bake at 350 degrees for 30 to 40 minutes, until bubbly. This may be made ahead, covered and frozen prior to baking; thaw in refrigerator for 24 hours before baking. Makes 10 to 12 servings.

Garlic French Bread

Brittany Cowan
Virginia, IL

This is a great, easy side that can go with about any meal!

3/4 c. butter, melted
1/4 t. onion powder

1/4 t. garlic salt
1 loaf French bread, sliced

In a bowl, stir together melted butter and seasonings. Brush butter mixture over both sides of each bread slice. Reassemble loaf on a piece of aluminum foil; wrap well. Place on a baking sheet. Bake at 350 degrees for 15 to 20 minutes, until bread starts to brown on the bottom. Makes 8 to 10 servings.

The true essentials of a feast are only fun and food.

-Oliver Wendell Holmes

122

Paprika Chicken

Mia Rossi
Charlotte, NC

My son Jason was reading Dracula, *and was intrigued when one character was served "paprika chicken" at an inn. He asked me if I could make it for him, so I searched until I found a recipe. It's now a family favorite, especially on Halloween!*

1 c. onion, chopped
2 T. butter
2 T. smoked paprika
1 T. all-purpose flour
14-1/2 oz. can whole tomatoes
Optional: 1 green pepper,
    chopped

1 t. salt
1/4 t. pepper
1-1/2 to 3 lbs. chicken
8-oz. pkg. goulash egg noodles,
    uncooked
8-oz. container sour cream
1 T. fresh parsley, chopped

In a large skillet over medium heat, sauté onion in butter until tender. Sprinkle with paprika and flour; cook and stir for one minute. Stir in tomatoes with juice, green pepper if using, salt and pepper. Add chicken pieces to skillet; turn to coat well. Cover and simmer for about 45 minutes, turning once, until tender and chicken juices run clear. About 20 minutes before serving time, cook noodles as package directs; drain and transfer to a serving platter. Arrange chicken pieces over noodles; cover to keep warm. Bring sauce mixture in skillet to a boil; stir in sour cream. Spoon sauce over chicken and noodles; sprinkle with parsley. Makes 4 servings.

Spread a cozy buffalo-check
blanket on the dining table...
instant comfort on a damp
and chilly day!

Vegetable Sauce with Spaghetti

Janet Sharp
Milford, OH

I like to make this very tasty sauce when I want to use up odds & ends of fresh vegetables in my fridge. It's easy to substitute any vegetables you may have on hand. Top with lots of cheese. Children love this dish too!

8-oz. pkg. spaghetti, uncooked
1 onion, chopped
1 clove garlic, chopped
3 T. olive oil
2 15-1/2 oz. cans diced
   tomatoes
1/2 lb. sliced mushrooms

1/2 lb. asparagus, cut into
   2-inch pieces
1 yellow pepper, sliced
1 t. dried parsley
1 t. dried basil
8-oz. pkg. favorite shredded
   cheese, divided

Cook spaghetti according to package directions; drain. Meanwhile, in a large skillet over medium heat, sauté onion and garlic in oil for about 5 minutes. Add tomatoes with juice; reduce heat to medium-low. Simmer for 15 to 20 minutes, stirring occasionally. Add remaining ingredients except garnish. Simmer for 5 to 7 minutes, until vegetables are just tender. Add cooked spaghetti to mixture in skillet; mix gently and warm through. Stir in 3 tablespoons cheese; remove from heat. Serve spaghetti and sauce topped with remaining cheese, as desired. Makes 6 servings.

Top decorative urns with plump pumpkins for a quick & easy doorstep welcome. Orange pumpkins are cheerful looking, or try white Lumina pumpkins for a ghostly appearance.

Baked Stuffed Shrimp & Crab

*Lori Rosenberg
University Heights, OH*

*Sometimes the group wants to upgrade the "eats" for the big game.
That's when I pull out this delicious recipe. It's such a favorite
that sometimes I make a double batch!*

1/2 lb. lump crabmeat, drained
   and flaked
1 c. finely shredded Swiss
   cheese
1/3 c. mayonnaise
2 T. dry bread crumbs

pepper to taste
24 uncooked jumbo shrimp,
   peeled, cleaned and
   butterflied
Garnish: lemon wedges

In a bowl, combine crabmeat, Swiss cheese, mayonnaise and bread
crumbs. Season with pepper; stir with a fork until well blended.
Arrange shrimp cut-side down on a lightly greased baking sheet with
tails curved over the top. Stuff one generous tablespoonful of crab
mixture into the center of each curled shrimp. Bake at 400 degrees for
10 to 12 minutes, until shrimp are pink and firm and stuffing is hot.
Serve with lemon wedges. Makes 6 to 8 servings.

Sometimes the simplest front door decorations are
the prettiest! Gather 5 or 6 brightly colored ears of
Indian corn by the dried husks and tie with a big ribbon bow.

Easy Herb-Roasted Turkey

Cathy Hillier
Salt Lake City, UT

My siblings and I take turns hosting our family's Thanksgiving dinner. As a newlywed, I was pretty worried when my turn rolled around, but I found this recipe and gave it a try. It turned out juicy and delicious...I was so proud!

10 to 12-lb. turkey, thawed
   if frozen
2 c. water
Optional: 1 apple and/or
   1 onion, quartered
3/4 c. olive oil

2 T. garlic powder
2 t. dried basil
1 t. dried sage
1 t. salt
1/2 t. pepper

Remove giblets package from turkey; pat turkey dry with paper towels. Place turkey in a roasting pan with a lid; add water to pan. If using, tuck apple and/or onion quarters into turkey. In a small bowl, mix oil and seasonings; brush over turkey. Bake, covered, at 325 degrees for 3 to 3-1/2 hours, brushing occasionally with oil mixture. If desired, uncover during the last 30 minutes to allow turkey to brown. Turkey is done when juices run clear and a meat thermometer inserted into the thickest part of one thigh measures 165 degrees. Remove turkey to a serving platter. Cover loosely with aluminum foil; let stand for 20 to 30 minutes before slicing. Makes 12 to 16 servings.

Homemade pan gravy is delicious and easy to make. Remove the turkey to a platter, then set the roaster with pan juices on the stovetop. Shake together 1/4 cup cold water and 1/4 cup cornstarch in a small jar; pour into the roaster. Cook and stir over medium heat until gravy comes to a boil and thickens, 5 to 10 minutes. Add salt and pepper to taste, and it's ready to serve.

Cranberry Bread Pudding, page 202

Crustless Bacon-Swiss Quiche, page 12

Spicy Pumpkin Waffles, page 15

Pumpkin Pie Smoothie, page 32

Cari's Ranch Cheese Ball, page 167

Pepper Poppers, page 149

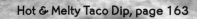
Hot & Melty Taco Dip, page 163

Caramel Apples, page 199

Creamy Chicken & Gnocchi Soup, page 45

Too-Easy Cherry Cobbler, page 212

Skinny French Dip Beef Sandwiches, page 65

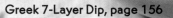
Greek 7-Layer Dip, page 156

Game-Day Chili Beer Brisket, page 130

Easy-Cheesy Stuffed Shells, page 121

Cranberry Relish, page 91

Pepperoni Pizza Burgers, page 63

Frosted Banana Bars, page 201

Speedy Tamale Pie, page 112

Creamy White Chicken Chili, page 37

Paprika Chicken, page 123

Grandmother's German Potato Salad, page 77

Navy Bean Soup, page 43

Turkey-Stuffed Shells

Rebecca Etling
Blairsville, PA

One of my favorite post-Thanksgiving recipes using leftover turkey!

12 jumbo pasta shells, uncooked
6-oz. pkg. chicken-flavored
   stuffing mix
4 c. cooked turkey or chicken,
   diced
8-oz. pkg. frozen peas, thawed
1 c. mayonnaise

salt and pepper to taste
Optional: 1/2 c. chopped onion,
   1/2 c. chopped celery
2 10-3/4 oz. cans cream of
   mushroom or chicken soup
1-1/4 c. water

Cook pasta shells according to package directions; drain. Prepare
stuffing mix according to package directions. In a bowl, combine
stuffing and remaining ingredients except soup and water. Fill shells
with stuffing mixture. Arrange shells in a greased 13"x9" baking pan.
Whisk together soup and water in a separate bowl; spoon over shells.
Bake, uncovered, at 350 degrees for 30 to 45 minutes. Makes 5 to
6 servings.

On Turkey Day, there's really no need for fancy appetizers...
just set out a bowl of unshelled walnuts or pecans and a
nutcracker! Guests will busy themselves cracking nuts to
snack on while you put the finishing touches on dinner.

Baked Ham with Brown Sugar Glaze

Claudia Keller
Carrollton, GA

This tender, sweet ham studded with pineapple chunks and cherries will be the prettiest dish at your holiday buffet!

8 to 10-lb. fully cooked
    semi-boneless ham
4 c. boiling water, as needed
1 c. brown sugar, packed
2 T. all-purpose flour
2 T. dry mustard

1/4 c. honey
20-oz. can pineapple chunks,
    drained and juice reserved
10-oz. jar maraschino cherries,
    drained

Place ham on a rack set in a roasting pan. Add 1/2 inch of boiling water to pan. Bake, uncovered, at 400 degrees for 2 hours, or until a meat thermometer inserted into the thickest part of ham reads 150 degrees. Remove from oven; reduce oven temperature to 350 degrees. In a bowl, combine brown sugar, flour, mustard and honey. Stir in enough of reserved pineapple juice to make a thick paste; stir until smooth. Brush glaze generously over ham; set aside. Insert a wooden toothpick into each pineapple chunk. Top each with a cherry and insert into ham, with cherries on top. Return ham to oven; bake for another 15 minutes. Brush ham and fruit with glaze and pan juices; bake for an additional 15 minutes. Remove ham to a serving platter; let stand 10 to 15 minutes before slicing. Makes 15 to 20 servings.

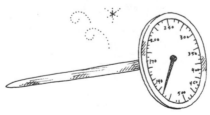

An instant-read meat thermometer is handy to check doneness. Recommended temperatures:

chicken and turkey = 165 degrees,
beef = 140 to 155 degrees,
pork = 150 to 160 degrees

Polynesian Pork

Glenna Kennedy
Ontario, Canada

I have been making this recipe for years...it's a delightful alternative to turkey over the holidays. It is so tasty and different, I've found even friends who don't care for pork love it. This recipe can be doubled for a crowd.

1-1/2 lbs. boneless pork chops,
    cubed
1/4 c. soy sauce
10-1/2 oz. can beef consommé
1/3 c. vinegar
1/4 c. brown sugar, packed
1-1/2 T. cornstarch
salt and pepper to taste

19-oz. can diced tomatoes
14-oz. can pineapple chunks,
    drained
1 onion, chopped
1/2 c. green pepper, cut into
    strips
cooked rice

In a large saucepan sprayed with non-stick vegetable spray, brown pork over medium heat. Meanwhile, in a small bowl, combine consommé, vinegar, brown sugar, cornstarch, salt and pepper. Stir until cornstarch is dissolved; add to pork and stir well. Add tomatoes with juice, pineapple, onion and green pepper; stir well. Cover and simmer over medium-low heat for about one hour, until pork is very tender. Serve over fluffy hot rice. Makes 4 to 6 servings.

Younger guests will feel so grown up when served bubbly sparkling cider or ginger ale in long-stemmed plastic glasses.

Game-Day Chili Beer Brisket

Cheri Maxwell
Gulf Breeze, FL

Mashed potatoes are a must with this flavorful slow-cooker beef.
Or spoon into slider buns for a wonderful tailgating item.

2-1/2 lb. beef brisket
1 t. salt
1 t. pepper
1/4 t. garlic powder
12-oz. jar chili sauce

1 onion, sliced
12-oz. can regular or
   non-alcoholic beer
Optional: chopped fresh
   parsley

Rub brisket all over with seasonings. Place brisket fat-side down in a
4-quart slow cooker. Spoon chili sauce over brisket; lay sliced onion
on top of brisket. Cover and cook on low setting for 6 hours, or until
brisket is very tender. Pour beer over brisket. Turn slow cooker to
high setting; cover and cook another 30 minutes. Remove brisket to
a serving platter. Let stand for 5 to 10 minutes; slice very thin. Serve
sliced brisket with hot cooking juices. Makes 6 to 8 servings.

Warm dinner rolls or sandwich buns for a crowd...easy!
Fill a roaster with rolls, cover with heavy-duty aluminum foil
and cut several slits in the foil. Top with several dampened paper
towels and tightly cover with more foil. Place in a 250-degree
oven for 20 minutes. Rolls will be hot and steamy.

Delicious Oven Bar-B-Que Ribs *Nancy Hanson*
Murrieta, CA

*I have been making these wonderful ribs for over 35 years now...
they never disappoint! They are not only delicious but oh-so easy
to prepare. Enjoy!*

4 lbs. pork spareribs or
   country-style ribs
1 c. catsup
1 c. water
1/3 c. vinegar
1/3 c. brown sugar, packed
3 T. Worcestershire sauce

1 t. dry mustard
1 t. paprika
1 t. salt
1/2 t. chili powder
1 onion, thinly sliced
1/2 lemon, thinly sliced

Place ribs in a Dutch oven; cover with water. Bring to a boil over high
heat; reduce heat to medium-low. Simmer until ribs are nearly tender,
about one hour. Drain ribs and place in a shallow baking pan; discard
cooking liquid. To a saucepan over medium heat, add remaining
ingredients except onion and lemon. Bring to a boil; cook and stir for
5 minutes. Stir in onion and lemon. Cool; spoon over ribs. Cover and
refrigerate up to 24 hours. Bake, uncovered, at 350 degrees for
45 minutes, basting often with pan juices. Makes 4 servings.

Today's Special:
- Pan-Fried Pork Chops
- Famous Mac & Cheese
- Strawberry Spinach
  Salad & Dressing
- Peachy Fruit
  Sorbet

For party menus, tried & true is best! Use simple recipes
you know will be a hit, rather than trying new recipes at
the last minute. Guests will be happy, and you'll avoid
tossing dishes that didn't turn out as expected.

Cranberry-Glazed Cornish Hens

Gladys Kielar
Whitehouse, OH

Let a grandmother's recipe feed your company! Cornish hens are perfect for the holiday table when you'd rather not roast a whole turkey. These tasty hens are stuffed with wild rice, so you only need to add a vegetable or a tossed salad for a delicious dinner.

4 22-oz. Cornish hens, thawed
6-oz. pkg. fast-cooking brown
   & wild rice mix
1/2 c. celery, sliced

Optional: 1/3 c. slivered almonds
8-oz. can jellied cranberry sauce,
   divided
2 T. olive oil, divided

Remove giblets package from hens; pat dry with paper towels. Place hens on a wire rack in a roasting pan; set aside. Prepare rice according to box directions. Stir in celery, almonds and half of cranberry sauce; let cool. Spoon about 3/4 cup rice mixture into each hen. Tie drumsticks together with kitchen twine. Brush some of the oil over hens. Bake, uncovered, at 425 degrees for 45 to 50 minutes, brushing occasionally with remaining oil. Hens are done when juices run clear and a meat thermometer inserted into the thickest part of hens measures 165 degrees. In a small saucepan, heat remaining cranberry sauce over low heat until melted. Remove hens to a serving platter; discard twine. Spoon cranberry sauce over hens. Makes 4 to 8 servings.

Roasted Cornish hens are a great choice for festive meals when just a few will be dining. Serve one hen per person for an impressive presentation, or halve hens after roasting for smaller appetites.

Harvest Dinner
Mains

Harvest Turkey Pot Pie

Janis Parr
Ontario, Canada

This is a fantastic dish to serve to company...quick to prepare and so comforting and delicious. There will be many requests for the recipe.

1/4 c. onion, chopped
1 T. butter
2 10-3/4 oz. cans cream of
   chicken soup
3 c. cooked turkey, cubed
2 McIntosh apples, peeled, cored
   and cubed

1/2 c. fresh cranberries
1 t. lemon juice
1/4 t. cinnamon
1/8 t. poultry seasoning
10-inch pie crust

In a large saucepan over medium heat, sauté onion in butter until tender. Stir in remaining ingredients except pie crust; simmer gently. Spoon turkey mixture into an ungreased 11"x7" baking pan. Roll out pie crust to a 12-inch by 8-inch rectangle. Place over filling in baking pan. Flute edges; cut several slits to vent. Bake at 425 degrees for 15 minutes. Reduce heat to 375 degrees; continue baking for about 35 minutes more, until crust is golden and filling is bubbly. Serve piping hot. Makes 6 servings.

What is a family, after all, except memories?
Haphazard and precious as the contents of
a catch-all drawer in the kitchen.

-Joyce Carol Oates

Oktoberfest Pork Stew

Vickie
Gooseberry Patch

This hearty stew will warm you right up on a chilly fall day!
Serve in bowls, ladled over mashed potatoes, with chunky
applesauce and pumpernickel rolls on the side.

1/3 c. all-purpose flour
1-1/2 t. salt
1/4 t. pepper
2 lbs. boneless pork roast,
   cut into 1/2-inch cubes
2 T. oil
3 to 4 onions, sliced 1/2-inch
   thick

1 clove garlic, minced
14-1/2 oz. can chicken broth
12-oz. can regular or
   non-alcoholic beer
2 T. red wine vinegar
1 T. brown sugar, packed
1 t. caraway seed
1 bay leaf

In a large plastic zipping bag, mix flour, salt and pepper. Add pork cubes; seal bag and shake until coated well. Heat oil in a Dutch oven over medium-high heat. Add pork and cook until browned on all sides, about 10 to 15 minutes. Add onions and garlic; cook and stir 5 minutes, until onions are soft. Stir in remaining ingredients; bring to a boil. Reduce heat to low. Cover and simmer for one hour, or until pork is very tender, stirring occasionally. Discard bay leaf just before serving. Makes 8 servings.

Just for fun, serve up soft pretzels instead of dinner rolls.
Twist strips of refrigerated bread stick dough into pretzel shapes
and place on an ungreased baking sheet. Brush with beaten
egg white; sprinkle with coarse salt and bake as directed.

Roast Pork Loin

Malacha Payton
Edmond, OK

*Perfect for company! This recipe gets rave reviews whenever
I serve it...your family & friends will love it too..*

3 to 4-lb. pork top loin roast
3 T. lemon juice
2 T. Dijon mustard
1/2 t. ground ginger
1/2 t. garlic salt

1 t. salt
14-1/2 oz. jar spiced apple rings,
   drained and syrup reserved
Garnish: fresh parsley sprigs

Place roast fat-side up in a roasting pan; set aside. In a bowl, combine
lemon juice, mustard and seasonings. Mix thoroughly and spread over
roast. Bake, uncovered, at 350 degrees for one to 1-1/2 hours. After
one hour, baste often with reserved apple syrup. Roast is done when a
meat thermometer inserted into thickest part of roast reads 145 degrees
for medium or 160 degrees for well-done. Remove roast to a serving
platter; let stand for 10 to 15 minutes before slicing. Garnish with
spiced apple rings and fresh parsley. Makes 6 to 8 servings.

Nothing says "autumn" like a warming mug of spiced apple cider!
Pour 2 quarts of cider into a saucepan and stir in 1/2 cup of red
cinnamon candies. Simmer over low heat, stirring constantly,
until hot and candies are dissolved, about 8 minutes.

Fun Fall Foods

Mexi-Mac Bowls

Amanda Walton
Marysville, OH

*A south-of-the-border twist on a classic chili-mac dish.
A little bit of spice that's perfect for a cold winter night. Comfort
food at its best...fast, easy and delicious!*

2 c. elbow macaroni, uncooked
1 lb. ground beef, chicken
   or turkey
1 yellow onion, chopped
1 green pepper, chopped
salt and pepper to taste
2 T. taco seasoning mix
2 c. favorite salsa

15-oz. can fire-roasted diced
   tomatoes
15-oz. can pinto beans, drained
   and rinsed
2 c. shredded Muenster cheese
1 c. shredded sharp Cheddar
   cheese
Garnish: sour cream

Cook macaroni according to package instructions; drain and return to
pan. Meanwhile, brown meat in a large skillet over medium heat.
When meat is almost done, add onion and green pepper; season lightly
with salt and pepper. When meat is browned, stir in taco seasoning
and cook for 3 minutes. Add salsa, tomatoes with juice and pinto
beans. Stir well; reduce heat to low and simmer for 5 to 10 minutes.
Add cheeses to hot cooked macaroni; stir until melted. Combine
macaroni mixture and meat mixture; mix thoroughly. Serve in bowls,
topped with a dollop of sour cream. Makes 6 servings.

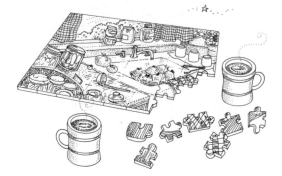

Family night! Serve a simple supper, then spend
the evening playing favorite board games or assembling
jigsaw puzzles together.

Spanish Stew & Cornbread

Barbara Imler
Noblesville, IN

I usually have all the ingredients for this recipe in the pantry and freezer, so when it's cold outside and I want something warm and filling, I can whip up this dish in almost no time. It keeps well in the fridge and makes great leftovers!

2 8-1/2 oz. pkgs. cornbread mix
1-1/2 lbs. ground beef chuck
1 onion, chopped
1 green pepper, chopped
16-oz. can chili beans
14-1/2 oz. can hot or mild diced
    tomatoes with green chiles
4-oz. can diced green chiles

15-1/4 oz. can corn, drained
8-oz. can tomato sauce
1/2 c. sliced green olives with
    pimentos
1/2 c. raisins
1-1/4 oz. pkg. taco seasoning
    mix
1/4 t. pepper

Using both mixes, prepare cornbread. Bake according to package directions in a 9" pie plate or a 9"x9" baking pan. Meanwhile, in a large skillet over medium heat, brown beef with onion and green pepper; drain. Stir in undrained chili beans, tomatoes and chiles; add remaining ingredients. Simmer over low heat for 10 minutes. Cut cornbread into 8 wedges or squares. To serve, place each piece of cornbread on a plate; ladle stew over cornbread. Makes 8 servings.

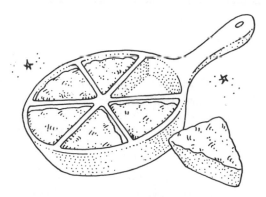

If you like your cornbread extra crisp, prepare it in
a vintage sectioned cast-iron skillet. Each wedge of
cornbread will bake up with its own golden crust.

No-Fuss Turkey & Stuffing

Charlene McCain
Bakersfield, CA

I love turkey & stuffing and like to have it more often than just holidays, but who has the time? With my slow cooker and prepared stuffing mix, my family and I can enjoy a scrumptious turkey dinner whenever we want. Pass the cranberry sauce, please!

1/2 c. onion, diced
1/2 c. celery, chopped
3 T. butter, divided
2 6-oz. pkgs. chicken-flavored
    stuffing mix

1/2 c. hot water
2 to 3-lb. boneless turkey breast
1/4 t. poultry seasoning
1/2 t. salt
1/2 t. pepper

In a skillet over medium heat, sauté onion and celery in one tablespoon butter, just until translucent. Meanwhile, lightly grease the inside of a 6-quart slow cooker. Spread dry stuffing mix in bottom of crock. Add onion mixture, water and remaining butter; mix well. Place turkey, breast-side up, on top of stuffing mixture; sprinkle with seasonings. Cover and cook on low setting for 6 hours, or until turkey juices run clear. Remove turkey breast from slow cooker to a cutting board. Let stand several minutes before slicing. Gently stir stuffing in crock; transfer to a serving platter. Top stuffing with sliced turkey. Makes 4 to 6 servings.

At Thanksgiving, my family literally had "Over the River and Through the Woods...to Grandmother's House we Go." Growing up in Tennessee, my parents' families lived close, so we were able to enjoy spending time with all of our family during the holidays. Thanksgiving was often at my Grandma Wahl's house. Everyone came, and we would play games and have the best time with all of my cousins. The traditional Thanksgiving dinner was served, and today I serve the same dishes when my family comes to me now. I want to carry on the traditions for many years to come!

-Karen VanLoo, Pflugerville, TX

Day-After-Thanksgiving Bake

Sena Horn
Payson, UT

This recipe is perfect for using up all the yummy Turkey Day leftovers, or easy to make with boxed stuffing mix and instant potatoes when you want a taste of Thanksgiving any time of the year! Delicious... even better served with turkey gravy and cranberry sauce on the side.

4 c. leftover stuffing, divided,
  or 2 6-oz. pkgs. chicken-
  flavored stuffing mix,
  prepared and divided
4 c. cooked turkey, coarsely
  chopped

1/4 c. whole-berry cranberry
  sauce
3/4 c. mayonnaise, divided
2 c. mashed potatoes
1-1/2 c. shredded Swiss cheese

Spray a 13"x9" baking pan with non-stick vegetable spray. Spoon in 2 cups prepared stuffing; top with turkey. In a small bowl, combine cranberry sauce and 1/4 cup mayonnaise; spread evenly over turkey. In a large bowl, combine remaining mayonnaise, mashed potatoes and cheese; spread over turkey. Top with remaining stuffing. Cover with aluminum foil. Bake at 375 degrees for 40 minutes, or until heated through. For a crisper top, remove foil during the last 10 minutes of baking. Allow to stand for 10 minutes before serving. Makes 6 servings.

Thanksgiving is so family-centered...why not host a post-holiday potluck with friends later in the weekend? Everyone can bring their favorite "leftover" concoctions, relax and catch up together.

Cheeseburger Meatloaf

Sherry Page
Akron, OH

This recipe is a keeper! Family & friends love my meatloaf. I get asked so often for my recipe that I keep extra copies with me. If I take this dish to a picnic, I add 1/2 cup chopped sweet pickles. The squares can also be served on buns.

10 saltine crackers, crushed
1-1/2 t. dried oregano
1-1/2 t. dry mustard
1-1/2 t. chili powder
1-1/2 t. dried parsley
1-1/2 t. Italian seasoning
1-1/2 t. dried basil
1-1/2 t. pepper
3 lbs. ground beef round

2 eggs, beaten
2 cloves garlic, minced
1/4 c. grated Parmesan cheese
10 slices American cheese,
   chopped
10 slices provolone cheese,
   chopped
Garnish: catsup

In a small bowl, mix crushed crackers and spices very well. In a large bowl, combine beef, eggs, cracker mixture, garlic and cheeses. Mix with both hands; shape mixture to fit a greased 8"x8" baking pan. With a wooden spoon handle, poke a hole in each corner and one in the center. Cover generously with catsup. Bake, uncovered, at 350 degrees for 1-1/2 to 2 hours, until beef is no longer pink in the center. Cut into squares. Makes 8 to 10 servings.

Keep little ones busy and happy with a crafting area while
the grown-ups put the finishing touches on Thanksgiving dinner.
Set out paper plates to decorate with colored paper, feathers,
pom-poms, crayons and washable glue. At dinnertime,
they'll be proud to display their creations!

Beef Boogie Woogie

Carol Geyer
Port Charlotte, FL

*This is an easy and simple slow-cooker take on Beef Bourguignon.
The aroma makes your whole house smell yummy.*

10-3/4 oz. can cream of
   mushroom soup
1/2 c. dry red wine or beef broth
1-1/4 oz. pkg. beefy onion
   soup mix

2 lbs. lean stew beef cubes
1/2 lb. baby carrots
1/2 lb. sliced mushrooms
cooked egg noodles

Whisk together soup, wine or broth and soup mix in a 4-quart slow
cooker until well blended. Add beef cubes, carrots and mushrooms; stir
until coated. Cover and cook on high setting for 4 hours, or on low
setting for 8 to 10 hours, until beef is very tender. Serve ladled over
cooked noodles. Makes 4 servings.

Twisty Bread Sticks

Lynn Williams
Muncie, IN

Perfect for dipping into saucy stews and savory sauces!

12 frozen dinner rolls, thawed
1/4 c. butter, melted

1/4 c. grated Parmesan cheese
Optional: garlic powder to taste

Roll each roll into a 16-inch rope. For each roll, twist each end in
opposite directions 3 to 4 times; pinch ends together. Place butter and
cheese in 2 shallow bowls. Dip each bread stick in melted butter and
then into cheese. Place bread sticks one inch apart on a baking sheet
sprayed with non-stick vegetable spray. Sprinkle with garlic powder,
if desired. Cover with sprayed plastic wrap; let rise until double in size.
Uncover; bake at 350 degrees for 15 to 20 minutes, until golden.
Makes one dozen.

Make herbed butter in a jiffy! Unwrap a stick of butter and cut in
half. Roll each half in chopped fresh herbs, then slice and serve.

Skillet Macaroni & Beef

Jeanne Caia
Ontario, NY

This is a tried & true recipe that my mother used to make for us when I was growing up. Now it is a favorite I make for my own family. A delicious, easy, one-pan weeknight dinner!

1 lb. ground beef
2 c. elbow macaroni, uncooked
1/2 c. onion, minced
1/2 c. green pepper, chopped
2 8-oz. cans tomato sauce

2 T. Worcestershire sauce
1/2 c. water
1 t. salt
1/4 t. pepper

Cook beef in a large skillet over medium heat until no longer pink. Using a slotted spoon, remove beef from skillet to a bowl; reserve drippings in skillet. Add uncooked macaroni, onion and green pepper to drippings in skillet. Cook until macaroni is golden, stirring often. Return beef to skillet along with remaining ingredients. Cover and simmer for 15 minutes, or until macaroni is tender. Makes 4 servings.

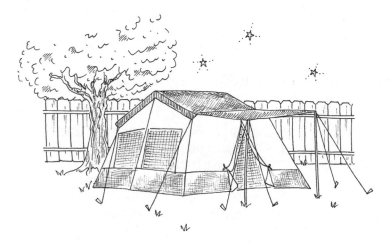

Pitch a tent in the backyard on a fall night so the kids can camp out, tell ghost stories and play flashlight tag. What a great way to make memories!

Zucchini Noodles & Meatballs

Courtney Stultz
Weir, KS

My in-laws had "Spaghetti Sundays" every week and our extended family would get together. It was always the same meal, but we really enjoyed our time together. But after I found out I was severely allergic to gluten, dairy, eggs and soy, the tradition came to a halt because it was a little hard to deal with. Finally I perfected this recipe...and now we can enjoy our dinners together again!

1 lb. ground turkey
2 T. plus 2 t. Italian seasoning, divided
5 T. olive oil, divided
4 tomatoes, chopped
6-oz. can tomato paste
1/2 c. water

1 T. white wine vinegar
4 zucchini, ends trimmed
1/8 t. sea salt
1/8 t. pepper
Optional: shredded Parmesan cheese

In a bowl, combine turkey and 2 tablespoons Italian seasoning. Blend well and form into one-inch meatballs. In a large skillet over medium heat, heat 2 tablespoons oil. Add meatballs. Cook on all sides for 5 to 8 minutes, until cooked through. Meanwhile, in a separate bowl, combine 2 tablespoons oil, remaining seasoning, tomatoes, tomato paste, water and vinegar. Stir until smooth; add more water for a thinner sauce, if desired. Add sauce to meatballs; simmer for about 2 minutes, until heated through. Use a spiralizer to make zucchini noodles, or shred zucchini lengthwise on the large holes of a box grater. Place zucchini strands in a separate skillet; drizzle with remaining oil and season with salt and pepper. Sauté over medium heat for about 5 minutes, just until tender. Place noodles on a serving plate; top with meatballs and sauce. Serve topped with shredded cheese, if desired. Makes 4 servings.

Making lots of meatballs? Grab a mini ice cream scoop or melon baller and start scooping...you'll be done in record time!

Prize-Winner Popover Pizza

Kristen Berning
Otsego, MN

More than 20 years ago, I won a Minnesota 4-H state cooking contest with this recipe, and later, 3rd place at the national contest. The judges couldn't believe how easy and practical it was! Everyone still loves this recipe, especially my three young children. If you prefer, use a jar of your favorite spaghetti sauce instead of the sauce mix, tomato sauce and water.

1-1/2 lbs. ground beef
1.35-oz. pkg. spaghetti sauce
   mix
15-oz. can tomato sauce
1/2 c. water
Garnish: sliced pepperoni,
   chopped onion, sliced
   mushrooms, sliced olives,
   diced peppers

8-oz. pkg. shredded mozzarella
   cheese
2 eggs
1 c. milk
1 T. oil
1/2 t. salt
1 c. all-purpose flour
grated Parmesan cheese
   to taste

Brown beef in a skillet over medium heat; drain. Stir in sauce mix, tomato sauce and water. Reduce heat to low; simmer until sauce is warm. Spoon beef mixture into a greased 13"x9" baking pan. Add pizza toppings as desired; sprinkle evenly with mozzarella cheese and set aside. In a separate bowl, beat eggs, milk, and oil with an electric mixer on low speed until well blended. Add salt and flour; mix together. Pour batter over beef mixture in pan. Sprinkle with Parmesan cheese, as desired. Bake at 400 degrees for 25 to 30 minutes. Slice into squares to serve. Makes 8 to 10 servings.

If lots of kids are coming for an after-game party, make it easy with do-it-yourself tacos or mini pizzas! Guests can add their own favorite toppings. Round out the menu with pitchers of soft drinks and a yummy dessert. Simple and fun!

Corned Beef Von Reuben

Deirdre Edgette
Lima, OH

My dear friend Phyllis gave me this recipe years ago and we still love it! We've been friends for a long time, since 7th grade.

6-oz. pkg. seasoned croutons, divided
12-oz. can corned beef, drained and crumbled
16-oz. can sauerkraut, drained
Optional: 1 T. caraway seed

8-oz. pkg. shredded Swiss cheese
3 eggs
2 c. milk
Garnish: Thousand Island salad dressing

Spread half of the croutons in a buttered 11"x7" baking pan. Layer with corned beef. In a bowl, mix sauerkraut with caraway seed, if using; spread evenly over corned beef. Layer with remaining croutons; top evenly with cheese. In a separate bowl, beat eggs with milk; pour over cheese layer. Bake, uncovered, at 350 degrees for 35 minutes, or until center is set and a knife tip tests clean. Serve with salad dressing on the side. Makes 6 to 8 servings.

Carve or drill a pattern of round holes in hollowed-out pumpkins, then set tealights inside for a flickering glow.

Hearty Hungarian Goulash

Amanda Johnson
Marysville, OH

This hearty soup or stew is a real hit with my family. My husband and our boys beg me to make it for them! It is great for warming up on brisk fall or winter days. Just add a basket of crusty bread.

2 t. shortening
2 onions, diced
1 lb. stew beef cubes
4 c. water
3 cubes beef bouillon, crushed
2 t. garlic, minced

3 T. paprika
1 to 1-1/2 t. cayenne pepper
salt and pepper to taste
2 bay leaves
4 russet potatoes, diced
Optional: chopped fresh parsley

Melt shortening in a skillet over medium heat. Add onions and sauté until softened. Add beef cubes; brown beef on all sides. Transfer beef mixture to a large stockpot over medium heat. Stir in water, bouillon, garlic and seasonings. Reduce heat to low; add bay leaves. Cover and simmer for 2 to 2-1/2 hours, stirring often, until beef is tender. Season with salt and pepper; add potatoes. Simmer an additional 40 to 45 minutes, until potatoes are tender but not mushy. Discard bay leaves. Ladle into soup bowls; garnish with parsley, if desired. Makes 4 servings.

If it's Thanksgiving now, Christmas can't be far away.
Why not double any must-have casseroles or stews and freeze half for a busy holiday weeknight...you'll be so glad you did!

Winning Touchdown

Touchdown

Appetizers

Slow-Cooker Chicken Nachos

Donna Wilson
Maryville, TN

My family loves this recipe and requests it often. It's easy to put together and tastes wonderful with tortilla chips.

12-oz. pkg. frozen chicken
  strips, thawed and cubed
16-oz. pkg. Mexican-style
  pasteurized process cheese,
  cubed
16-oz. can black beans, drained

1 c. salsa
8-oz. container sour cream
8-oz. pkg. frozen green peppers
  and onions, thawed
tortilla chips

In a 4 to 6-quart slow cooker coated with non-stick vegetable spray, combine chicken, cheese, beans and salsa. Cover and cook on low setting for one hour. Stir in sour cream and green pepper mixture. Turn slow cooker to high setting. Cover and cook for one more hour, stirring occasionally. Serve with tortilla chips. Makes 8 servings.

I remember my brother, sister and my 8-year-old self getting ready to walk in the annual Halloween parade. Our mother didn't have money to buy costumes, so she would conjure up the best homemade garb. The long, gathered skirt, big dangling earrings, long necklaces and colorful scarf would transform me into a "gypsy" ready to gather goodies on that Halloween. I still love it! Now, while everyone else is basking in the hot sunshine of June, I'm counting down to fall. "Only four months until Halloween!" I say to anyone who will listen. Maybe it's the hopeful anticipation of cool weather finally coming our way or the excitement of the coming holidays spent with family & friends. I believe it's both, mixed with the feelings of thankfulness for all the blessings we have been given. I love fall!

- Paula Anderson, Kingwood, TX

Pepper Poppers

Clara Honeyager
Waukesha, WI

These are so yummy...this is my family's favorite appetizer!
Whenever I bring them for snacks, they're gone in 30 minutes.

1 lb. bacon
1-1/2 c. cream cheese, softened
1/4 t. garlic powder
1/4 t. salt
12 jalapeño peppers, halved and
   seeds removed

1 c. shredded Cheddar or
   Monterey Jack cheese
1/2 to 1 c. dry bread crumbs
Optional: ranch salad dressing
   or sour cream

In a large skillet over medium heat, cook bacon until crisp; drain well
and crumble. Meanwhile, add cream cheese to a large bowl. Blend in
seasonings; add crumbled bacon and mix well. Spoon 2 tablespoons
cheese mixture into each pepper half. If any cheese mixture is left,
divide among peppers. Put bread crumbs in a shallow dish. Roll
peppers in bread crumbs; place on a lightly greased baking sheet.
If making ahead, cover with aluminum foil and refrigerate. Bake,
uncovered, at 350 degrees for 30 to 35 minutes, until bubbly
and golden. Serve with salad dressing or sour cream, if desired.
Makes 2 dozen.

When making any dish with hot peppers as an ingredient,
it's always a good idea to wear a pair of plastic gloves to
protect your skin while slicing or chopping the peppers.

Fun Fall Foods

Sausage Bread

Jennifer Wilken
Bourbonnais, IL

To make this recipe super fast, I use already-cooked sausage crumbles. Not only does it save time, but there's one less pan to wash. This can be made ahead and baked at party time. Just keep it chilled in the fridge to prevent the dough from rising.

16-oz. pkg. frozen bread dough
10-oz. pkg. ready-to-use
   sausage crumbles
1/2 c. onion, diced
1 green, red, yellow or orange
   pepper, diced
2 c. favorite shredded cheese

Thaw bread dough in the refrigerator. On a floured surface, roll out dough into a rectangle, 1/2 to 3/4-inch thick. In the center of the rectangle, layer remaining ingredients, leaving a 2-inch border on all sides. Fold over the sides first, then the ends; press to seal. Place seam-side down on a greased baking sheet. Bake at 375 degrees for about 30 minutes. Cool slightly; slice. Makes 10 to 12 servings.

Bacon & Cheddar Bubble Bread

Sharon Murray
Lexington Park, MD

Need a little extra for the party table? This is quick and tasty.

11-oz. tube refrigerated
   dinner rolls
1 T. bacon bits
1/2 c. finely shredded
   Cheddar cheese

Cut each roll into quarters; set aside. Mix bacon bits and cheese in a bowl. Toss roll pieces in cheese mixture until lightly coated. Place in a greased 13"x9" baking pan. Bake at 350 degrees for 20 to 25 minutes, until top is deeply golden. Run a knife around edge of bread to loosen; lift onto a serving plate. To serve, pull apart pieces of rolls from bread loaf. Makes 4 to 6 servings.

Mini Corn Dog Muffins

Joyceann Dreibelbis
Wooster, OH

This is a great party appetizer for guests! It's easy and fun to make...only takes about 20 minutes to prepare.

8-1/2 oz. pkg. corn muffin mix
24 1/2-inch cubes Cheddar
    cheese or pasteurized
    process cheese

4 beef or turkey hot dogs,
    each cut into 6 pieces
Garnish: savory honey mustard

Prepare corn muffin mix as directed on package; spoon batter into 24 mini muffin cups sprayed with non-stick vegetable spray. Press one cheese cube and one hot dog slice into the center of each muffin cup. Bake at 375 degrees for 10 to 12 minutes, until golden. Let muffins cool for 5 minutes before removing from pan. Serve warm with mustard. Makes 2 dozen.

Throw a pumpkin painting party. Provide acrylic paints, brushes and plenty of pumpkins...invite kids to bring their imagination and an old shirt to wear as a smock. Parents are sure to join in too!

Spiced-Up Turkey Roll-Ups

Nancy Kailihiwa
Wheatland, CA

We think traditional turkey rolls are too bland, but these have just the right amount of spice. They're a great finger food to make a day ahead for a less-stress party day. Be prepared to share this recipe!

8-oz. pkg. cream cheese, softened
4-oz. can green chiles, drained
1 avocado, peeled, pitted and cubed
4 burrito-size flour tortillas

12 slices deli roast turkey
2 c. lettuce, shredded
1 c. carrot matchsticks, chopped
1-1/2 c. shredded Pepper Jack cheese

In a bowl, combine cream cheese, green chiles and avocado. Beat with an electric mixer on low speed until well mixed and smooth. Spread evenly on tortillas. Arrange 3 turkey slices per tortilla on cream cheese mixture. Add a thin layer of shredded lettuce on turkey followed by carrot bits. Top with shredded cheese. Roll up tortillas tightly; place on a plate and wrap in plastic wrap. Chill overnight for best results. At serving time, trim the ends off each roll and discard. Slice each roll into 6 to 7 slices. Makes about 2-1/2 dozen.

The secret to being a relaxed hostess...choose foods that can be prepared in advance. At party time, simply pull from the fridge and serve, or pop into a hot oven as needed.

Parmesan Cheese Ball

Shirley Howie
Foxboro, MA

This is an old standby recipe that I use for holiday party buffets. It is very easy to make and everyone really likes it! I like to use both walnuts and pecans, but you can use all of one or the other. Serve the cheese ball on a platter, surrounded by a variety of crackers.

2 8-oz. pkgs. cream cheese,
   softened
2/3 c. grated Parmesan cheese
2/3 c. walnuts, finely chopped
1/4 c. onion, finely chopped

1 T. milk
1/4 t. garlic powder
1/2 t. salt
1/4 t. pepper
1/2 c. pecans, coarsely chopped

In a large bowl, combine all ingredients except pecans. Stir together until well blended. Shape into a ball; roll in pecans to coat. Wrap cheese ball in plastic wrap; refrigerate for at least 8 hours or overnight. Let stand at room temperature about 30 minutes before serving. Makes 12 servings.

For tasty fun at the next tailgate party, turn any favorite cheese ball recipe into a "football." Just shape, sprinkle with paprika and pipe on cream cheese "laces"...so easy!

Sticky Honey Chicken Wings

Liz Plotnick-Snay
Gooseberry Patch

You'll want plenty of napkins for these tasty wings! Like it hot?
Just add a shake of hot pepper sauce. Sometimes we'll use
chicken drumsticks when an extra-hungry crowd will be coming.

2-1/2 lbs. chicken wings,
   separated
Optional: salt to taste
pepper to taste
1/2 c. honey

1/2 c. soy sauce
2 T. catsup
1/2 t. garlic powder
1/2 t. ground ginger

Cover a shallow baking pan with heavy-duty aluminum foil; coat with non-stick vegetable spray and set aside. Lightly season chicken wings on all sides with salt, if desired, and pepper. Arrange chicken wings in pan. Bake at 425 degrees for 20 minutes. Meanwhile, whisk together remaining ingredients in a bowl. Remove wings from oven; drain. Spoon or brush sauce over wings. Return to oven for another 20 to 25 minutes, turning wings over in sauce every 5 minutes, until well glazed and chicken juices run clear. Makes about 10 servings.

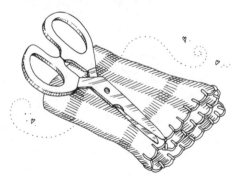

Wondering what's the best way to cut up slippery chicken wings? A pair of sturdy kitchen scissors does the job in a jiffy. Afterwards, wash the scissors well in soapy water and set on a towel to dry.

Raspberry Balsamic-Glazed Meatballs

Wendy Ball
Battle Creek, MI

As a diabetic, I've been looking for easy, tasty low-sugar recipes that I'd be able to enjoy at potluck functions. This recipe fills the bill! If that's not a concern, just substitute regular preserves and sugar.

2 16-oz. pkgs. frozen meatballs
1 c. low-sugar or sugar-free
  raspberry preserves
3 T. calorie-free powdered
  sweetener

3 T. balsamic vinegar
1-1/2 T. Worcestershire sauce
Optional: 1/4 t. red pepper flakes
1 T. fresh ginger, peeled and
  grated

Add meatballs to a 3 to 4-quart slow cooker coated with non-stick vegetable spray; set aside. In a microwave-safe bowl, combine preserves, sweetener, vinegar, sauce and red pepper flakes, if using. Microwave on high for 45 seconds; stir. Microwave an additional 15 seconds or until melted, as needed. Reserve 1/2 cup of preserves mixture; refrigerate. Spoon remaining preserves mixture over the meatballs; toss to coat. Cover and cook on low setting for 4 to 5 hours. Turn slow cooker to high setting; stir in ginger and reserved preserves mixture. Cook, uncovered, another 15 to 20 minutes, or until sauce is thickened slightly. Makes about 2-1/2 dozen.

It's not how much we have, but how much
we enjoy, that makes happiness.

-Charles Haddon-Spurgeon

Greek 7-Layer Dip

Nola Coons
Gooseberry Patch

Our tailgating crowd was getting a little bored with layered Mexican dip, so when I ran across this recipe, I gave it a try. This taste of the Mediterranean scored a touchdown with everyone!

8-oz. container chives & onion
   cream cheese spread
8-oz. container hummus
1 cucumber, peeled and chopped
3 to 4 roma tomatoes, chopped
2-1/4 oz. can sliced black olives,
   drained

4-oz. container crumbled feta
   cheese
4 green onions, chopped
pita chips or white corn
   tortilla chips

Spread cream cheese spread evenly in a 10" glass pie plate or serving dish. Drop hummus by small spoonfuls over cream cheese; spread evenly. Top with remaining ingredients except chips in order listed. Serve with pita or tortilla chips. Makes 15 servings.

Every October since my children were small, they would go to the local apple orchard and pick Melrose apples with my dad. They would pick the biggest apples they could find. Every school year, one lucky teacher would be the recipient of a huge Melrose apple. Then we would have a caramel apple party for all the kids in the neighborhood. Everyone got to decorate their own apple with caramel, chocolate, candies and whatever else we could find. My kids have both grown up and my father is no longer with us, but I still pick apples and remember the good times we had.

-Sue Gibson, Louisville, OH

White Bean Dip with Sun-Dried Tomatoes

Carole Rhoades
Galena, OH

This appetizer is a yummy way to get your protein, fiber and healthy oils all in one.

15-oz. can cannellini beans, drained and rinsed
1/4 c. extra-virgin olive oil
4 marinated sun-dried tomatoes
2 cloves garlic, minced
1 t. onion powder
1/2 t. fresh rosemary, chopped
1/4 t. kosher salt
1/4 t. pepper
1/8 t. cayenne pepper
Garnish: chopped fresh chives
pita chips

Combine all ingredients except garnish and pita chips in a blender. Process until smooth; transfer to a serving bowl. Garnish with chives; serve with pita chips. Makes 6 to 8 servings.

Hollow out a speckled turban squash and fill with a favorite dip for veggies or chips...a fall twist on a serving bowl!

Fun Fall Foods

Mushroom-Cheese Pinwheels

Mary Bettuchy
Columbia, SC

I make these every year for Thanksgiving...they must be on the table! My sister Sarah loves them so much she makes them every year too. She lives across the country from me, so we don't often get to celebrate the holidays together. This recipe joins us together on Thanksgiving, as we both have it on our tables! They are even good eaten cold right out of the fridge.

2 T. butter
1/2 lb. mushrooms, very finely minced
2 cloves garlic, minced
1 shallot, minced
1 t. dried thyme
1/2 c. red wine or beef broth
salt and pepper to taste
1 sheet frozen puff pastry dough, thawed
4-oz. container spreadable cheese with garlic & fine herbs, softened

Melt butter in a large skillet over medium heat. Add mushrooms, garlic, shallot and thyme. Sauté for about 5 minutes, until vegetables are soft and starting to turn golden. Add wine or broth. Over low heat, simmer until liquid has almost completely evaporated, stirring occasionally, about 10 minutes. Remove from heat. Season with salt and pepper; set aside. On a lightly floured surface, gently roll out puff pastry to 1/8-inch thick. Spread cheese over pastry, leaving a 1/2-inch border on all 4 sides. Spread mushroom mixture over cheese layer. Roll up pastry jelly-roll style, pinching seam to seal well. Slice into rounds 3/4-inch thick. Place on a parchment paper-lined baking sheet. Bake at 375 degrees for about 20 minutes, until puffed and golden. Serve warm. Makes 4 servings.

Make a fabric garland. Cut strips of fabric, about 6 inches long and 1/2 inch wide, and a piece of thick jute the length you'd like the garland to be. Tie on the fabric strips with a simple knot. Try team colors for a tailgating party or orange and black for Halloween!

Mini Stuffed Peppers

Karen Brigham
Waterloo, NY

I made these colorful peppers for a big football party and they were a big hit. Reserve at least two peppers for yourself, as they will be gone quickly!

1 lb. mini sweet peppers, halved and seeds removed
1 lb. ground pork sausage, browned and drained

1-1/2 c. cream cheese, softened
1/2 t. garlic powder
1/2 t. onion powder

Add peppers to a saucepan of boiling water. Boil for 4 minutes; drain on paper towels. Combine remaining ingredients in a bowl. Spoon mixture into pepper halves, filling 1/2 full. Place on an ungreased baking sheet. Bake at 375 degrees for 15 minutes, or until golden and peppers are fork-tender. Makes about 4 dozen.

Cheese-Stuffed Mushrooms

Bobbie Metzger
Pittsburgh, PA

This recipe was given to me by a wonderful cook years ago. It's the first thing my boys ask for on special occasions.

8-oz. pkg. cream cheese, softened
1 c. grated Parmesan cheese
1/4 c. whipping cream

1/2 t. garlic salt
24 large mushrooms, stems removed
1/2 c. butter, melted

In a bowl, combine cheeses, cream and garlic salt; blend well. Fill mushroom caps with cheese mixture. Dip bottoms of mushrooms into melted butter; place on an ungreased baking sheet. Bake at 350 degrees for 15 minutes, or until lightly golden. Makes two dozen.

Warm Cranberry Tea Punch

Lynda Robson
Boston, MA

From Halloween until Christmas, guests at my home are greeted with a warm mug of this cheerful punch. It's become a real favorite! Try different flavors of spiced tea for variety.

4 c. water
8 tea bags
2 c. unsweetened cranberry juice
2 c. apple juice
4-inch cinnamon stick

4 whole cloves
1/2 t. ground ginger
1/2 c. brown sugar, packed
Garnish: additional cinnamon
  sticks, orange slices

In a large saucepan, bring water to a boil over high heat. Remove from heat; add tea bags and steep for 5 to 10 minutes. Discard tea bags. Add juices, cinnamon stick, whole cloves and ginger. Cover; simmer gently over low heat for 5 minutes. Add brown sugar; cook and stir until dissolved. Discard whole spices. Serve in mugs, garnished with a cinnamon stick and an orange slice. Makes 8 to 10 servings.

Slow cookers are oh-so-handy party helpers. They're super
for keeping spiced cider or cranberry punch simmering
or cheesy appetizers piping-hot too.

Harvest Moon Golden Punch

Shannon Reents
Loudonville, OH

This time of year, I like to use autumn colors in everything, even the food and beverages I serve! This yummy punch is easy to change for the holiday. Just use orange gelatin mix for Halloween, red strawberry for Christmas and so forth. Enjoy!

6-oz. pkg. lemon gelatin mix
3/4 c. sugar
2 c. hot water
46-oz. can unsweetened
    pineapple juice

12-oz. can frozen lemonade
    concentrate, thawed
4 ltrs. lemon-lime soda, chilled

In a large bowl, dissolve gelatin mix and sugar in hot water. Add pineapple juice and lemonade. Mix well; pour into a freezer container. Cover and freeze. Shortly before serving time, remove from freezer; add to a punch bowl and let thaw slightly. Add desired amount of chilled soda; stir gently. Makes 15 to 20 servings.

Create a pumpkin man to greet visitors. Stack up 3 pumpkins snowman-style, removing stems and trimming bottoms as needed so they sit flat. Add twig arms and a whimsical face...fun!

Mini Spinach Frittatas

Carolyn Deckard
Bedford, IN

These little morsels are delicious and a cinch to make. The recipe doubles easily for a crowd and even freezes well...something quick & easy to add to the snack tray.

24 slices pepperoni
1 c. ricotta cheese
3/4 c. grated Parmesan cheese
10-oz. pkg. frozen chopped
    spinach, thawed and
    squeezed dry

2/3 c. mushrooms, chopped
1 egg, beaten
1/2 t. dried oregano
1/4 t. salt
1/4 t. pepper

Place a slice of pepperoni in each of 24 greased mini muffin cups; set aside. In a small bowl, combine remaining ingredients; blend well. Fill muffin cups 3/4 full with cheese mixture. Bake at 375 degrees for 20 to 25 minutes, or until a toothpick inserted in the center comes out clean. Carefully run a knife around edges of muffin cups to loosen. Serve warm. Makes 2 dozen.

An instant appetizer that's always a hit! The ingredients can even be kept on hand for guests who pop in. Unwrap a block of cream cheese and place it on a serving plate. Top with zesty salsa, spicy pepper sauce or fruity chutney. Serve with crisp crackers and a cheese spreader.

Hot & Melty Taco Dip

*Stephanie D'Esposito
Ravena, NY*

This dip is a must make for our family parties. My friend Christy says she wants to dive into it and eat the whole thing!

16-oz. can refried beans
1-1/2 oz. pkg. taco seasoning
   mix
16-oz. container sour cream
8-oz. pkg. cream cheese,
   softened
16-oz. jar salsa

8-oz. pkg. shredded sharp
   Cheddar cheese
1/2 head lettuce, shredded
Optional: sliced black olives,
   jalapeño peppers, green
   onions, chopped tomatoes
tortilla chips

In a bowl, combine refried beans with taco seasoning. Spread in the bottom of a lightly greased 13"x9" glass baking pan; set aside. In a separate bowl, blend sour cream and cream cheese; spread over bean layer. Pour salsa over sour cream layer; sprinkle cheese on top. Bake, uncovered, at 350 degrees for about 25 minutes, until cheese is melted and beans are warmed through. Top with shredded lettuce and other desired toppings. Serve with tortilla chips. Makes 8 servings.

Freaky-face pizza snacks! Lightly toast English muffin halves, spread with pizza sauce, and sprinkle with cheese. Make a face with toppings such as pepperoni and black olive "eyes," carrot curl "hair" and green pepper "smiles."

Sweet-and-Sour Chicken Wings

Diana Krol
Nickerson, KS

Spicy-hot and delicious...perfect at a party or as a main course family meal. I find that using an electric skillet gives you really good control of the heat, and you can do a lot of wings quickly.

3 lbs. chicken wings, separated
1 t. salt
1 c. cornstarch
4 eggs, beaten
corn oil for deep frying
1/2 c. sugar

1/2 c. vinegar
1/2 c. jalapeño pepper jelly
1/4 c. soy sauce
3 T. catsup
2 T. lemon juice

Season chicken wings with salt; set aside. Place cornstarch and eggs in 2 shallow bowls. Roll wings first in cornstarch, then in beaten eggs. Add 2 inches oil to an electric skillet or regular skillet over medium-high heat; heat to 370 degrees. Add wings to oil, a few at a time. Fry for several minutes, until crisp and golden on all sides. Drain wings on paper towels; transfer to an ungreased 15"x10" jelly-roll pan. In a separate saucepan, mix together remaining ingredients. Stirring constantly, bring to a boil over medium heat. Reduce heat to low and simmer for 10 minutes. Pour hot sauce over wings. Bake wings, uncovered, at 350 degrees until glazed, 20 to 30 minutes. Makes 10 to 12 servings.

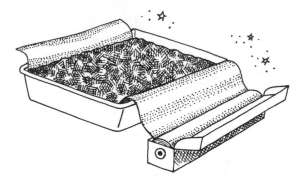

When baking sticky chicken wings or saucy meatballs, be sure to cover the baking pan with heavy-duty aluminum foil, then spray with non-stick vegetable spray. No sticking, no clean-up!

JJ's Beer Meatballs

Janine Jackson
Page, AZ

I have made these meatballs for over 40 years, and never had a bad review. You can't eat just one! They taste a bit like sweet-and-sour meatballs. I have to double or triple this recipe for my family. It is very good served over pasta too.

2 lbs. lean ground beef, or
    32-oz. pkg. frozen
      homestyle meatballs
14-oz. bottle catsup

12-oz. can regular or
    non-alcoholic beer
1 c. sugar

Roll beef into one-inch balls; add to a large skillet over medium heat. Brown on all sides; drain well and set aside. If using frozen meatballs; omit this step; simply thaw. In a Dutch oven over medium heat, combine catsup, beer and sugar. Cook and stir until sugar is dissolved. Add meatballs; reduce heat to low. Cover and simmer for 30 to 40 minutes, stirring occasionally, until sauce thickens. Transfer meatballs with sauce to a serving bowl. Serve with small plates and a container of toothpicks. Makes 8 to 12 servings.

That first crackling fire and scent of wood smoke tell us
it's fall! Gather lots of games and puzzles for cozy nights
at home with family & friends.

Scotch Eggs

Myrtle Miller
Providence, KY

Make these hearty eggs for a special breakfast at home, or pack in a picnic basket for a camping trip or tailgating party.

6 to 8 eggs, hard-boiled, peeled
   and well chilled
1 lb. ground pork sausage
1/2 t. dried sage
1/2 t. pepper

1/4 c. all-purpose flour
2 eggs, well beaten
1/2 to 3/4 c. dry bread crumbs
oil for deep frying

Prepare eggs ahead of time; set aside. Combine sausage, sage and pepper in a large bowl. Mix well; divide into 6 to 8 portions. Press sausage mixture around chilled hard-boiled eggs, retaining the oval shape. Sprinkle eggs with flour, coating lightly on all sides. Place beaten eggs and bread crumbs in 2 shallow bowls. Dip into beaten eggs; roll in bread crumbs. Heat about 2 inches oil in skillet. Fry prepared eggs until golden; drain. Transfer eggs to an ungreased baking sheet. Bake at 350 degrees for 5 to 10 minutes. Remove from baking pan; drain in a colander or on paper towels. Serve hot or cold, whole or sliced in halves. Makes 6 to 8 whole eggs or 12 to 16 half-eggs.

Do you love tailgating but can't score tickets to the big stadium football game? Tailgating at the local Friday-night high school game can be just as much fun...round up the gang, pack a picnic and cheer on your team!

Cari's Ranch Cheese Ball

Carilee Daniels
Newport, MI

One of my most-requested church potluck recipes! I have also changed it up a little by rolling the cheese ball in real bacon bits or seasoned dry bread crumbs. The flavor is best if made a day in advance, so it's a good make-ahead.

3 8-oz. pkgs. cream cheese,
   softened
2 1-oz. pkgs. ranch salad
   dressing mix
2 T. grated Parmesan cheese
2 T. Worcestershire sauce

1/2 c. onion, chopped
1/4 c. green pepper, diced
8-oz. pkg. shredded sharp
   Cheddar cheese
crackers, pretzels, chips or
   sliced vegetables

In a large bowl, combine cream cheese, ranch dressing mix, Parmesan cheese, Worcestershire sauce, onion and green pepper. Use a potato masher or spoon to mix very well. Form cheese mixture into a ball; roll in shredded Cheddar cheese to coat. Wrap in plastic wrap; refrigerate 24 hours, until set. Let stand at room temperature about 15 to 20 minutes before serving. Serve with crackers, pretzels, chips or vegetables for dipping. Makes 15 to 20 servings.

Paper muffin cup liners come in all colors and even seasonal designs...great for serving individual portions of snacks and party mix.

Speedy Southwestern Corn

Lisa Robason
Corpus Christi, TX

Served with tortilla chips, this is an awesome hot tailgating dip! It's also a great spicy side dish on its own. For even more heat, leave the seeds in the jalapeños.

2 15-1/4 oz. cans corn, drained
8-oz. pkg. cream cheese,
   softened
2 T. milk
4-oz. can diced green chiles
2 jalapeño peppers, diced and
   seeds removed
1 red pepper, diced
1/4 c. red onion, chopped

1/2 t. ground cumin
1/2 t. chili powder
1/4 t. garlic powder
1/4 t. salt
1/4 t. pepper
1/8 t. cayenne pepper
Optional: shredded Monterey
   Jack cheese

Place corn in a large microwave-safe bowl. Add remaining ingredients except optional shredded cheese. If desired, top with shredded cheese. Microwave on high for 30 seconds; stir. Microwave for another 30 seconds; mix thoroughly. If needed, heat again for 30 seconds, until everything is blended. Transfer to a serving bowl. Makes 10 to 12 servings.

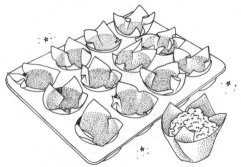

Serve your favorite yummy hot or cold dip spooned into crisp wonton cups...so easy, yet so impressive on an appetizer tray! Coat a muffin tin with non-stick vegetable spray, then press a wonton wrapper gently into each cup. Spritz with a little more spray and bake at 350 degrees for 8 minutes, or until golden. Fill as desired.

Uncle Pickle & Aunt T's Favorite Tomatillo Salsa

Rebecca Gonzalez
Moreno Valley, CA

This is a salsa my best friends and I love! We live far from each other now, but when we get together, I make sure I have plenty of this salsa on hand to enjoy with chips. Enjoy it as a condiment too.

12 tomatillos, husks removed
1 onion, peeled and quartered
3 to 4 serrano chiles, to taste

3 to 4 cloves garlic, peeled
salt to taste

Add all ingredients except salt to a large saucepan; cover with water. Bring to a boil over high heat; reduce heat to medium. Boil for 15 minutes, or until tomatillos start to split open. With a slotted spoon, remove all ingredients and add to a blender. Process until smooth; season with salt. Cool before serving; cover and keep refrigerated. Makes 12 to 15 servings.

Serve homemade tortilla chips with your favorite salsa! Simply cut corn tortillas with seasonal cookie cutters. Spritz cut-outs with non-stick vegetable spray and arrange on an ungreased baking sheet. Sprinkle with salt and bake at 350 degrees until crisp, 5 to 10 minutes.

Apricot Kielbasa Bites

Mary Patenaude
Griswold, CT

Need a change from sausage with chili sauce & grape jelly?
Try this, it's delicious! Sure to be a hit at any party.

1 lb. Kielbasa sausage, sliced
   1/4-inch thick
12-oz. jar apricot preserves

2 T. lemon juice
2 t. Dijon mustard
1/4 t. ground ginger

In a skillet, brown Kielbasa over medium-high heat; drain and set aside. Add remaining ingredients to skillet; cook over low heat for 2 to 3 minutes, stirring occasionally. Return Kielbasa to skillet. Cook over low heat for 5 to 6 minutes, stirring occasionally, until heated through. Makes about 4 dozen.

Kielbasa & Apples

Veronica Richards
San Antonio, TX

The first time I tasted this recipe was 20 years ago. It's absolutely
wonderful and perfect for autumn.

2 lbs. Kielbasa sausage, sliced
   1/8-inch thick
4 21-oz. cans apple pie filling

1 t. cinnamon
1/2 t. allspice

Brown Kielbasa in a skillet over medium-high heat; drain and set aside. Add pie filling to a 4 to 6-quart slow cooker. Stir in Kielbasa and spices. Cover and cook on low setting for 3 to 4 hours. Makes 10 to 12 servings.

Wake up a Halloween snack platter with some surprising apple smiles! Cut apples into thin wedges. Spread peanut butter on one side of each wedge, then pair wedges with mini marshmallows in between for "teeth."

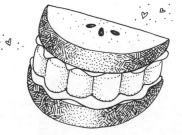

Winning Touchdown
Appetizers

Bacon Delights

Melisa Hesser
Lima, OH

This appetizer is for all you bacon-lovers out there. My kids all ask for this for every get-together...I never have any left!

1/2 c. catsup	2 T. water
1/4 c. brown sugar, packed	8-oz. can sliced water chestnuts,
1/4 c. steak sauce	drained
2 t. Worcestershire sauce	1 lb. thin-sliced bacon, halved

In a saucepan over medium-low heat, combine catsup, brown sugar and sauces. Simmer, stirring often, until brown sugar is dissolved. Remove from heat; stir in water and set aside. Place one slice water chestnut on each half-slice of bacon and roll up; secure with a wooden toothpick. Arrange in a well greased 13"x9" baking pan; spoon warm sauce over all. Bake, uncovered, at 400 degrees for 12 to 15 minutes, until bacon is crisp and sauce is gooey. Best served at room temperature. Serves 10 to 12.

Cheddar Cheese Puffs

Joyceann Dreibelbis
Wooster, OH

These cheesy appetizers are so easy to make and so quick to bake. A warm batch makes a savory snack or an appealing addition to a soup lunch.

1 c. shredded Cheddar cheese	1/4 c. butter, softened
1/2 c. all-purpose flour	1/2 t. dry mustard

Combine all ingredients in a bowl; mix well. Roll into one-inch balls. Place at least one inch apart on an ungreased baking sheet. Bake at 400 degrees for 12 to 15 minutes, until lightly golden. Best served warm. Makes about 2 dozen.

Classy Clam Dip

Stacie Perdue
Flemington, NJ

Perfect for parties! I've brought this dip to so many different events, including New Year's Eve and football get-togethers. It reheats well, so I often double the recipe and freeze half for the next fun occasion.

2 6-1/2 oz. cans minced clams
2 T. lemon juice
1/2 c. butter, sliced
1/2 onion, minced
1 t. garlic, minced
1 t. hot pepper sauce
2 T. dried parsley
2 T. dried oregano
1/8 t. pepper
3/4 c. seasoned dry bread
  crumbs
Garnish: 2 to 3 T. grated
  Parmesan cheese,
  1/8 t. paprika
snack crackers

Add clams with clam juice and lemon juice to a saucepan. Cover and simmer over low heat for 5 minutes. Add butter, onion, garlic, hot sauce and seasonings; simmer for another 5 minutes. Remove from heat. Add bread crumbs and stir until mixture reaches the consistency of oatmeal. Transfer to a lightly greased 2-quart casserole dish. Sprinkle with Parmesan cheese and paprika to taste. Bake at 350 degrees for 20 minutes. Serve warm with crackers. Makes 8 servings.

The next time a party guest asks, "How can I help?" be ready with an answer! Whether it's picking up a bag of ice, setting the table or even bringing a special dessert, friends are usually happy to lend a hand.

Special Seafood Spread

Julie Shenkle
Dubois, PA

When my husband and I got engaged, the young couples at our church threw us a recipe shower and this is one of the recipes we received. I have been making it for more than 20 years now.

2 8-oz. pkgs. cream cheese
4-1/4 oz. can crabmeat, drained
   and flaked
4-oz. can small shrimp, drained
2 T. prepared horseradish

1-oz. pkg. Italian salad
   dressing mix
1-1/2 T. lemon juice
1-1/2 t. onion, grated
round buttery crackers

Place cream cheese in a serving bowl; soften to room temperature. Add crabmeat and shrimp; mash with a fork and mix into cream cheese. Add remaining ingredients except crackers; mix well. Cover and refrigerate several hours to overnight. Serve with crackers. Makes 2 cups.

Party fun! Fill a big jar with pieces of candy corn...don't forget to count them first. Ask everyone to guess how many pieces are in the jar...send the jar home with the person whose guess is the closest!

Chicken-Fried Steak Fingers

Kay Marone
Des Moines, IA

When we hosted a tailgating party for my husband's friends, he had just one request...none of those "girlie" appetizers! Well, I think these crispy, beefy steak strips met his expectations pretty well..they were gone in a hurry!

2 eggs, beaten
3 T. milk
2 c. seasoned dry bread crumbs
1 t. salt
1/2 t. pepper

1-1/2 lbs. beef flank steak,
  sliced into thin strips
oil for frying
Garnish: red steak sauce,
  horseradish sauce

Whisk together eggs and milk in a shallow bowl; set aside. Combine bread crumbs and seasonings in a separate bowl. Dip beef strips into egg mixture, then into crumb mixture, coating well. Heat 2 tablespoons oil in a skillet over medium-high heat until very hot. Add beef strips, a few at a time; fry until golden and cooked to desired doneness. Drain on paper towels. Serve warm with sauces for dipping. Makes about 4 dozen.

Spice up your favorite ranch salad dressing. Into one cup
of dressing, whisk in 1/2 teaspoon ground cumin
and 1/4 teaspoon chili powder. Let stand a few minutes
for flavors to blend. Divine for dipping!

Beer-Battered Broccoli Bites

Jo Ann
Gooseberry Patch

You can make all kinds of tasty veggie appetizers with this batter. Cauliflower flowerets are good, but also try slices of zucchini and yellow squash and whole mushrooms. The sky's the limit!

1 c. self-rising flour
2 T. grated Parmesan cheese
1/4 t. garlic powder
1/4 t. onion powder
1/4 t. pepper

1 c. regular or non-alcoholic beer
4 c. broccoli flowerets
oil for deep frying
Garnish: ranch salad dressing

In a large bowl, whisk together flour, cheese, seasonings and beer until smooth. Add broccoli flowerets to batter; toss until well coated. In a heavy saucepan, heat 2 to 3 inches oil to 375 degrees. Add broccoli in batches; fry for 2 to 3 minutes, turning once, until golden. Drain on paper towels. Serve warm with salad dressing for dipping. Makes 8 to 10 servings.

I grew up back in the 1960s in a neighborhood where the streets were lined with big old trees. The best part was when the leaves would start falling and we could play in them. The neighborhood kids would all be out there raking the leaves, making huge piles of them to jump into. We all spent hours outside having fun with the leaves and just enjoying being kids. There wasn't anything like computers or video games to drag us into the house...
it was fun, free entertainment!

-Karla Himpelmann, Morris, IL

Nuts & Bolts

Denise Neal
Castle Rock, CO

This is a favorite from a wooden box of recipes my sister-in-law Miranda gave me. The recipes are handwritten and yellowed with age, just the way I like them. I've never seen this version of this snack before. It's great to heap up in a large bowl for games or holiday parties.

3 c. butter
1-1/2 T. Worcestershire sauce
1-1/2 t. garlic salt
1-1/2 t. onion salt
12-oz. pkg. bite-size crispy
　wheat cereal squares
12-oz. pkg. bite-size crispy
　rice cereal squares

12-oz. pkg. bite-size crispy
　corn cereal squares
9-oz. pkg. shredded wheat
　crackers
6-oz. pkg. thin pretzel sticks,
　rings or mini twists
1 c. peanuts or other nuts,
　as desired

In a large saucepan over low heat, melt butter with Worcestershire sauce and spices. Stir well; remove from heat. In an ungreased large roasting pan, combine remaining ingredients. Drizzle butter mixture over cereal mixture; toss to coat well. Bake, uncovered, at 225 degrees for 2 hours, stirring every 20 minutes. Stir well; cool before serving. Store in a covered container. Makes 15 to 20 servings.

Mummy's the word! Whip up some fun treat containers in a jiffy. Glue wiggly eyes to the front of plastic drink cups, then wind cotton gauze around & around, fastening at both ends with a little glue. Clever!

Winning Touchdown
Appetizers

Bucket o' Dirt Snack Mix

Erin Brock
Charleston, WV

Kids will love this tasty snack...it'll make them giggle too!
Pack in small pails for a fun take-home gift.

4 c. crispy chocolate rice cereal
    squares
1/4 c. butter, sliced
2 T. instant chocolate pudding
    mix

8 chocolate sandwich cookies,
    coarsely chopped
1 to 2 c. gummy worm or
    bug candies

Place cereal in a large microwave-safe bowl; set aside. Place butter in a microwave-safe 2-cup glass measuring cup. Microwave on high for one minute; stir in dry pudding mix. Pour over cereal mixture; stir until evenly coated. Microwave on high for 2 minutes. Stir in crushed cookies; add candies and toss to mix. Spread on wax paper to cool. Store in an airtight container. Makes 12 servings.

"Bloody" Halloween Punch

Donna Wilson
Maryville, TN

Don't be alarmed...it's just fruit punch! A realistic looking
and yet very tasty way to serve a Halloween punch. Use a
large glass beaker as a pitcher for a fun effect.

3 to 4 tubes red decorating gel
1 qt. pomegranate juice, chilled
1 qt. cranberry-apple juice,
    chilled

2 qts. lemon-lime soda, chilled
Optional: ice cubes

Squeeze gel around rims and down sides of glasses and a one-gallon pitcher. Combine juices and soda in pitcher; stir. Carefully pour into glasses. Add ice, if desired. Makes 16 servings.

Sweet invitations! Decorate paper gift bags with Halloween stickers and paint... write details on one side of bag. Later, bags can be used for collecting treats!

Dangerously Addictive Spiced Nut Mix

Sheri Kohl
Wentzville, MO

The name says it all! My brother-in-law Steve requests this every year for his birthday and then hides it from everyone until he finishes eating the whole bowl! You may want to double it.

1/4 c. butter, sliced
1 c. sugar
1-1/2 t. pumpkin pie spice
1/2 t. cinnamon
1/2 t. allspice

1/2 t. ground ginger
1/2 t. salt
2 c. salted dry-roasted peanuts,
    or a mix of peanuts, whole
    almonds and/or pecan halves

Combine all ingredients in a heavy skillet over medium heat. Cook, stirring constantly, until sugar is melted and golden, coating nuts, about 15 minutes. Spread nuts in a thin layer on aluminum foil-lined rimmed baking sheets. Cool completely; break into clusters. Store in an airtight container. Makes 6 to 8 servings.

Share chills & thrills with a monster movie night. Make a big batch of a favorite snack mix, let the kids each invite a special friend and scatter plump cushions on the floor for extra seating. Sure to be fun for everyone!

Warm Rum Apple Dip

Jenna Hord
Mount Vernon, OH

So easy to make...perfect for cozying up next to the fire.

8-oz. pkg. chopped pecans
2 11-oz. pkgs. butterscotch
  chips
3 T. light rum or 1 T. rum
  extract

Optional: 2/3 c. evaporated milk
4 to 5 Gala apples, cored and
  sliced

Lightly toast pecans in a skillet over low heat until golden. In a 2-quart slow cooker, combine pecans, butterscotch chips, rum or extract and milk, if desired for a creamier dip. Cover and cook on high setting, stirring often, just until chips are melted. Turn to low setting for serving, stirring often. Serve warm with sliced apples. Makes 3 cups.

Smoky Pumpkin Seeds

Courtney Stultz
Weir, KS

At our house, we love carving pumpkins and roasting the seeds from our pumpkins. This recipe is a great grown-up version for Halloween party snacking.

1 to 2 T. olive oil
1 c. pumpkin seeds
1 t. garlic salt
1/4 t. chipotle pepper

1/4 t. paprika
1/4 t. smoke-flavored cooking
  sauce

Drizzle an aluminum foil-covered pan with oil. Add pumpkin seeds to pan; sprinkle with remaining ingredients. Stir seeds on pan with a fork until coated in oil and spices. Bake, uncovered, at 350 degrees for about 25 minutes, stirring after 12 minutes. Let cool before serving. Makes one cup.

Whip up a jolly Jack-o'-Lantern shake! In a blender, combine
3 scoops vanilla ice cream, 2 tablespoons canned pumpkin,
1/4 cup milk and 1/4 teaspoon pumpkin pie spice. Blend until
smooth. Pour into tall glasses and share with a friend.

Pumpkin Spice Caramel Popcorn

Kim Hinshaw
Cedar Park, TX

*There's nothing better than the smell of pumpkin pie in the fall!
There are no caramel candies in this recipe...you're making
caramel from scratch, and it's easy to do.*

10 c. air-popped popcorn, salted
1 c. brown sugar, packed
1/4 c. light corn syrup
6 T. butter, melted

2 T. water
1/2 t. salt
1/2 t. baking soda
1-1/2 to 2 t. pumpkin pie spice

Line a rimmed baking sheet with parchment paper; set aside. Coat a large bowl with non-stick vegetable spray. Add popcorn to bowl and discard any unpopped kernels; set aside. In a heavy saucepan, whisk together brown sugar, corn syrup, butter, water and salt. Bring to a simmer over medium-high heat. Continue to simmer, whisking often; bring to a boil. Allow mixture to boil for about 2 minutes, whisking occasionally. Immediately remove from heat; whisk in baking soda and spice. Quickly pour the hot caramel mixture over popcorn. Use a rubber spatula to gently fold caramel into popcorn, mixing as evenly as possible. Spread popcorn mixture on baking sheet. Bake, uncovered, at 200 degrees for one hour, stirring and turning mixture with a spatula every 15 minutes. Spread out onto a separate wax paper-lined baking sheet. Allow to cool completely; store in an airtight container. Makes 10 cups.

Look for mini enamelware pails in bright home-team colors...
they're perfect for filling with crunchy party mixes!

Peanut & Pretzel Bark

Ramona Wysong
Barlow, KY

I love the sweet & salty taste of this candy.

24-oz. pkg. white melting
  chocolate, broken up
3 c. thin pretzel sticks,
  coarsely broken

3 c. salted dry-roasted
  peanuts

Line a rimmed baking sheet with parchment or wax paper; set aside. Place chocolate in a microwave-safe 2-quart glass dish. Microwave on high for one minute; stir. Microwave on high for one more minute; stir until chocolate is melted and smooth. If necessary, microwave on high for 10 seconds more; stir. Add pretzel pieces and peanuts; stir well with a flexible spatula. Spoon onto baking sheet; spread out mixture so that ingredients are evenly distributed. Allow to cool and set for several hours, until firm. Break bark into irregular pieces like peanut brittle. Store in an airtight container. Makes 16 servings.

My kids would help me plant pumpkin seeds and we'd watch them grow all summer. One year, I added mini pumpkins to the mix, planning to use them in my harvest decorations. While attending my son Jeremy's school open house, I noticed that there was a mini pumpkin on each desk. How cute, I thought, until his teacher thanked me for donating the pumpkins. The next day, when I checked my garden, I had to laugh. Jeremy had left just four pumpkins...one for each family member!

-Lori Schwander, North East, MD

Sweet Apple Nachos

Teree Lay
Sonora, CA

Apple picking at Sierra Glen Apple Ranch for our family's annual autumn gathering, hayrides, hot cider and apple spice cookies after a picnic lunch. Couldn't get much easier! Be sure to eat these with your hands...just like real nachos!

3 to 4 Honey Crisp apples, cored
   and thinly sliced
1 t. lemon juice
3 T. creamy natural peanut
   butter
1/4 c. sliced almonds

1/4 c. chopped pecans
1/4 c. unsweetened flaked
   coconut
1/4 c. mini semi-sweet chocolate
   chips, or more to taste

Lightly coat apple slices with lemon juice to keep them from browning too fast. Arrange apples on a serving platter; set aside. Place peanut butter in a microwave-safe cup. Microwave for a short time, until very runny; drizzle 2/3 of peanut butter all over apples. Top with nuts, coconut and chocolate chips. Drizzle with remaining peanut butter. Serve immediately. Makes 4 servings.

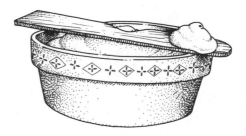

Looking for an alternative to peanut butter? Try sun butter, made from sunflower seeds, or soy nut butter, made from soybeans. If your child has a peanut allergy, check with the doctor first, to be on the safe side.

County Fair
Sweets & Treats

Miss Kay's Apple-Cranberry Dessert

Linda Caisse
Albuquerque, NM

I'm always making up recipes. I love to cook and have won over a hundred ribbons at the New Mexico State Fair. This is an original recipe that's perfect for this time of year...I hope you'll enjoy it!

2 12-oz. pkgs. fresh cranberries, thawed if frozen
2 c. Gala or Granny Smith apples, peeled, cored and chopped
3/4 c. plus 2 T. butter, divided
2-1/4 c. sugar, divided
3/4 c. chopped walnuts or pecans
2 eggs, lightly beaten
3/4 c. all-purpose flour
Garnish: vanilla ice cream or whipped cream

Grease the bottom of a 13"x9" baking pan. Add cranberries and apples to pan; toss to mix. Dot with 2 tablespoons butter. Sprinkle evenly with 1-1/4 cups sugar and chopped nuts; set aside. Melt remaining butter; cool slightly. In a bowl, whisk together eggs, melted butter, remaining sugar and flour. Mix well; pour batter evenly over cranberry mixture. Bake, uncovered, at 325 degrees for one to 1-1/2 hours, until golden on top. Serve warm or at room temperature, topped with ice cream or whipped cream. Makes 9 to 12 servings.

Be sure to pick up a couple pints of ice cream in pumpkin, cinnamon and other delicious seasonal flavors when they're available...they add that special touch to holiday meals!

Blue-Ribbon Pumpkin Bread

Joyceann Dreibelbis
Wooster, OH

No one will guess they're eating lighter when you serve moist slices of this pretty pumpkin bread with a ribbon of cream cheese inside. This was a first-place winner at our local county fair.

1 c. canned pumpkin
1/2 c. unsweetened applesauce
1 egg, beaten
2 egg whites, beaten
1 T. olive oil
1-2/3 c. all-purpose flour

1 c. sugar
1 t. baking soda
1/2 t. cinnamon
1/2 t. ground cloves
1/3 c. chopped walnuts

Make Cream Cheese Filling; set aside. In a large bowl, combine pumpkin, applesauce, egg, egg whites and oil; blend well. In a separate bowl, combine flour, sugar, baking soda and spices; add to pumpkin mixture and mix well. Stir in walnuts. Set aside half of batter. Divide remaining batter between 2, 8"x4" loaf pans coated with non-stick vegetable spray. Divide filling evenly between pans; top with reserved batter. Bake at 350 degrees for about 40 minutes, until a toothpick inserted near the center tests clean. Set pans on a wire rack for 10 minutes; turn out bread onto rack to cool completely before slicing. Refrigerate leftovers. Makes 2 loaves.

Cream Cheese Filling:

2/3 c. low-fat cream cheese, softened
1/4 c. sugar

1 T. all-purpose flour
2 egg whites, beaten

Combine all ingredients in a bowl; stir until smooth.

A wrapped loaf of homemade bread tied to a wooden cutting board makes a heartwarming gift.

Elephant Ears

Beth Bundy
Long Prairie, MN

Kids can help make these cinnamony pastries...it's a perfect way to get them into the kitchen! Unlike the county fair treats, these are baked, not deep-fried.

1 c. all-purpose flour
6 T. sugar, divided
1/2 t. baking powder
1/2 t. salt

1/3 c. milk
4 T. butter, melted and
   cooled slightly
1 t. cinnamon

In a bowl, combine flour, 2 tablespoons sugar, baking powder and salt. Stir in milk and 3 tablespoons melted butter until dough forms. Turn out dough onto a floured surface. Knead 10 times; roll out dough into a 9-inch by 5-inch rectangle. Brush with remaining butter. Mix 3 tablespoons sugar and cinnamon; sprinkle over dough. Roll up dough tightly, beginning on one short side. Pinch edges to seal. Slice rolled dough into 4 equal pieces with a very sharp knife. Place pieces cut-side up on a greased baking sheet; pat each into a 6-inch circle. Sprinkle with a little sugar. Bake at 425 degrees for about 8 to 10 minutes, until golden. Immediately remove to a wire rack; cool. Makes 4 servings.

A fun party theme...carnival time! Have cones of kettle corn for nibbling, followed by midway favorites like corn dogs, roasted corn on the cob, lemonade, funnel cakes and ice cream.

Apple Puffs

Eleanor Dionne
Beverly, MA

These little fritters are yummy! I like to make them when I want a sweet treat. Feel free to try your own favorite baking apple.

1 c. all-purpose flour
1/2 c. sugar
1 T. baking powder
1 c. Cortland apples, peeled,
   cored and chopped

1 egg, beaten
2/3 c. milk
oil for frying
Garnish: cinnamon-sugar
   or powdered sugar

In a bowl, mix flour, sugar, baking powder and apples. Add egg and milk; stir well. Heat 1/4 to 1/2 inch oil in a deep fryer or skillet over medium-high heat. Drop batter into hot oil by heaping tablespoonfuls. Cook until puffs are golden. Drain on paper towels. While still warm, roll fritters in cinnamon-sugar or powdered sugar. Makes 6 to 8 servings.

Years ago, my husband and I, along with our three children, lived on Long Island, New York. Every September, we would drive out east to an apple orchard to pick apples and pumpkins. We would also take my parents along with us. This particular orchard offered as many pumpkins as one person could carry for five dollars. We used to laugh and giggle so much as we piled pumpkins into my husband's arms, sometimes as many as ten pumpkins of all sizes, large and small. All the while, the children would be gathering apples, my mom planning her apple pies, and I would be setting up days to make applesauce. We still often talk about this special time in our lives.

-Rosemary Trezza, Tarpon Springs, FL

School Lunch Peanut Butter Bars

Sharon Jones
Fountain, FL

Remember the great-tasting peanut butter bars in the school lunchroom? This is it! I searched & searched, finally getting this recipe from a school lunchroom manager a few years ago. Yummy!

16-oz. pkg. graham crackers, crushed
2 T. butter, room temperature
1-1/2 to 2 16-oz. jars creamy peanut butter

16-oz. pkg. powdered sugar, divided

In a bowl, gradually mix cracker crumbs, butter and enough peanut butter to make a stiff mixture. Set aside 1/4 cup powdered sugar. Add remaining powdered sugar, a little at a time, to peanut butter mixture, using your hands. to mix. Press mixture 1/2-inch thick onto a wax paper-lined baking sheet. Sprinkle with reserved powdered sugar. Cover and refrigerate for about one hour. Cut into one-inch squares. Cover tightly and refrigerate for several days, or wrap and freeze for up to 2 months. Makes 2 dozen.

Caramel-Cinnamon Graham Crackers

JoAnn

Such an easy treat to whip up when you just need a little something!

24 cinnamon graham crackers, divided
1/2 c. butter, softened

1/2 c. margarine, softened
1 c. light brown sugar, packed
1 c. chopped pecans

Arrange a single layer of graham crackers on an aluminum foil-lined 15"x10" jelly-roll pan. Set aside. In a saucepan over medium-low heat, combine butter, margarine and brown sugar. Bring to a boil; cook for 2 minutes. Stir well and pour over crackers. Sprinkle nuts on top. Bake at 350 degrees for 12 minutes. Cut into triangles. Makes 4 dozen.

Ooey-Gooey Chewy Brownies

Debbi Bender
Hendersonville, NC

No one will ever guess these brownies have no flour in them! At Halloween and Christmas I make them festive by adding chocolate-coated candies in seasonal colors. Stir in extra chocolate chips or nuts, if you like.

1-1/2 c. semi-sweet chocolate
    chips
2-oz. sq. white melting
    chocolate, chopped
1/2 c. butter
1 c. sugar

1/3 c. baking cocoa
1 t. salt
1 t. baking powder
4 eggs
1 t. vanilla extract

Line an 11"x7" baking pan with aluminum foil; spray with non-stick vegetable spray and set aside. In the top of a double boiler, combine chocolates, butter and sugar. Cook over simmering water until chocolates melt, at least 10 minutes. Mixture will look smooth but have a grainy texture. With a whisk, stir in cocoa and salt; mix well. Remove from heat; whisk in baking powder. Whisk in eggs, one at a time, and vanilla until combined. Pour into pan. Bake at 350 degrees for 40 minutes. Remove from oven; let cool for about 10 minutes. Turn brownies out of pan; cut into bars. Makes 15 servings.

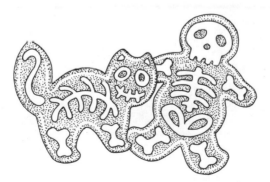

Serve up a batch of skeleton cookies for Halloween! Bake a batch of your favorite gingerbread men. After the cookies are baked and cooled, add "skeletons" using white frosting and a decorator tip. So clever!

Popcorn S'mores Bars

Beth Flack
Terre Haute, IN

*Mom used to make these fun marshmallow bar treats
for us as a twist on the usual s'mores.*

10 c. popped popcorn
10-1/2 oz. pkg. mini
   marshmallows
1 c. brown sugar, packed
1/2 c. butter, sliced
1/2 c. light corn syrup

1/2 t. baking soda
2 c. mini teddy bear-shaped
   graham cookies or mini
   graham squares
1 c. mini milk chocolate chips

Place popcorn in a roaster pan or heatproof bowl; discard any
unpopped kernels. Add marshmallows; toss to mix and set aside. In a
heavy saucepan, combine brown sugar, butter and corn syrup. Cook
over high heat for 5 minutes. Remove from heat; stir in baking soda.
Pour brown sugar mixture over popcorn mixture; stir to coat well.
Stir in graham cookies and chocolate chips. Press into a greased
9"x9" baking pan. Let stand for 15 minutes before cutting into squares.
Makes one dozen.

Choose a crisp fall evening to gather friends around a crackling
campfire. Serve hot cocoa and cookies, toast marshmallows,
tell ghost stories and watch smoke spiraling up as the evening
goes by...could there be anything cozier?

Popcorn Balls

Vickie
Gooseberry Patch

*A must for Halloween parties! For a double-corny treat,
add some candy corn to the popcorn mixture.*

16 c. popped corn	1-1/2 c. light corn syrup
1 T. butter	1/2 t. salt
1 c. sugar	1 t. vanilla extract

Place popcorn in a roaster pan; discard any unpopped kernels and set
aside. Melt butter in a saucepan over medium-low heat. Increase heat
to medium; add sugar, corn syrup and salt. Bring to a boil. Cook until
mixture reaches the hard-ball stage, or 250 to 269 degrees on a candy
thermometer. Stir in vanilla. Pour hot mixture over popped corn;
stir to coat well. Cool slightly; shape handfuls of mixture into balls
with buttered hands. Wrap individually in plastic wrap. Makes about
one dozen.

In my large suburban neighborhood, all the kids would get
together at the beginning of October to plan our Halloween
costumes. Everything was homemade. With our imaginations
and a little help from our moms, we'd turn out everything from
robots to witches, vagabonds to fairy princesses. Pumpkin carving
was an elaborate process the day before Halloween. We'd
transform some good-sized Jack-o'-Lanterns into ghoulish or silly
faces, and save the pumpkin seeds for roasting. On Halloween
night, we would eat a hurried dinner and head out
at dusk to start our candy adventure. With a dad or two in tow,
we'd run from house to house, our paper shopping bags in hand,
with cries of "Trick-or-treat!" as we greeted each neighbor. When
we returned home, we'd spill our "loot" onto the living room
carpet and sort through the piles. My dad would always steal a
candy bar, which was his tradition. By the end of the evening,
we were happy and content, knowing that in days ahead, school
lunches would always have a sweet treat to eat at the end!

- Maria Kuhns, Crofton, MD

One-Bowl Pumpkin Cake

Alice Dotterweich
Ringwood, NJ

A delicious Bundt® cake recipe from my late mother-in-law,
perfect for the autumn months or any time you crave pumpkin.
Can be mixed by hand, if you don't feel like dragging out the mixer!

4 eggs
2 c. sugar
1 c. canola oil
2 c. all-purpose flour
2 t. baking soda
1/2 t. salt
2 t. cinnamon

1 t. ground ginger
1 t. nutmeg
15-oz. can pumpkin
Optional: cream cheese frosting
 and chopped walnuts,
 or whipped cream and
 cinnamon

Lightly grease and flour a Bundt® pan or tube pan; set aside. In a large bowl, beat eggs with sugar and oil. Stir in flour, baking soda, salt and spices. Add pumpkin and mix well. Pour batter into pan. Bake at 350 degrees for 1-1/2 hours, or until cake tests done with a toothpick inserted near the center. Do not open oven door while baking. Remove from oven. Set pan on a wire rack for 15 minutes; turn out cake onto rack to finish cooling. Frost as desired and sprinkle with walnuts, or serve cake slices topped with whipped cream and dusted with cinnamon. Makes 12 servings.

Wow guests with a pumpkin-shaped cake. Place one Bundt® cake upside-down on a cake stand. Place a second cake right-side up on top and secure with frosting. Ice with orange frosting.

Mom's Apple Kuchen

Jennifer Zacher
Ontario, Canada

My mom's been making this yummy apple dessert forever. It's probably the only thing she ever bakes these days, and she doesn't make it often. But when autumn comes around, we like to visit nearby farms and pick apples...then we know there's a scrumptious Apple Kuchen to follow!

3/4 c. butter, softened
3/4 c. sugar
3 eggs, beaten
2 T. lemon juice
2 t. vanilla extract

1-1/4 c. all-purpose flour
6 McIntosh apples, peeled,
   cored and sliced
2 T. cinnamon

In a large bowl, combine all ingredients except apples and cinnamon. Stir together with a wooden spoon until well mixed. Spread batter onto a greased and floured 13"x9" baking sheet. Evenly arrange apples over batter in rows, touching or overlapping slightly as desired. Sprinkle apples with cinnamon and Sugar Topping. Bake at 350 degrees for 45 to 55 minutes, until golden on the edges and bottom. Remove from oven; let cool and cut into squares. Store at room temperature, covered with a tea towel. Makes 12 to 15 servings.

Sugar Topping:

1-1/2 c. all-purpose flour
1 c. sugar

1 T. vanilla extract
1 c. butter, softened

Combine all ingredients in a bowl; mix until crumbly.

For delicious apple desserts, some of the best apple varieties are Granny Smith, Gala and Jonathan.

Black Forest Ice Box Cake

Stephanie Turner
Meridian, ID

This creamy, chocolatey dessert is perfect for a warm Indian summer day when you want cake, but don't want to turn on the oven. The kids can even help arrange the cookies. Yum!

8-oz. pkg. cream cheese, room
   temperature
3.9-oz. pkg. instant devil's food
   or chocolate pudding mix
1-1/3 c. plus 1/2 c. milk, divided
1/2 c. powdered sugar
1-1/2 c. frozen whipped topping,
   thawed

14.3-oz. pkg. chocolate
   sandwich cookies, divided
1 c. chocolate syrup, divided
21-oz. can cherry pie filling,
   divided

Place cream cheese in a large bowl; beat with an electric mixer on medium-low speed until smooth. Add dry pudding mix and 1-1/3 cups milk; beat on low speed until smooth. Mix in powdered sugar. With a spatula, fold in whipped topping; set aside. Dip half of the cookies in some of remaining milk for about 5 seconds each; arrange in the bottom of a 9"x9" baking pan. Spread half of cream cheese mixture over cookies. Drizzle with one to 2 tablespoons chocolate syrup; spread with half of pie filling. Repeat layering with remaining cookies and milk, cream cheese mixture, syrup and pie filling. Drizzle with remaining syrup. Cover and refrigerate at least 4 hours to overnight. Makes 8 to 10 servings.

Make a tabletop Halloween tree. Choose a branch from the backyard. Spray it black and stand it securely in a weighted vase. Wind with twinkling lights...trim with tiny ghosts made of white hankies and mini Jack-o'-Lanterns. Boo!

194

Pam's Banana Split Brownie Pizza

Carolyn Deckard
Bedford, IN

We were looking for a great dessert to serve at a bridal shower, and my daughter remembered her mother-in-law serving this one at her shower. It was so delicious, everyone wanted the recipe!

20-oz. pkg. chewy fudge
   brownie mix
8-oz. pkg. cream cheese,
   softened
8-oz. can crushed pineapple,
   drained and juice reserved
2 T. sugar

2 ripe bananas, sliced
2 to 3 t. lemon juice
1 c. fresh strawberries, hulled
   and sliced
1 c. chopped nuts
Garnish: chocolate syrup

Prepare brownie mix according to package directions, using a greased 15" round pizza pan. Bake at 350 degrees for 20 minutes. Remove from oven; cool. Meanwhile, in a bowl, beat together cream cheese, pineapple and sugar. Add reserved pineapple juice as needed to make a good spreading consistency. Spread cream cheese mixture over cooled crust. Toss banana slices with lemon juice; drain. Arrange banana and strawberry slices over cream cheese mixture. Sprinkle with nuts and drizzle with chocolate syrup. Cover and refrigerate until serving time. To serve, cut into wedges. Makes 8 to 10 servings.

Do you have lots of kids coming for an after-game party or trick-or-treat night? Make it easy with do-it-yourself tacos or mini pizzas...guests can add their own favorite toppings. Round out the menu with pitchers of soft drinks and a yummy dessert pizza. Simple and fun!

Crazy Donut Hole Shish-Kabobs

Lisa Robason
Corpus Christi, TX

We like to make these fun kabobs for different holidays! Colors and designs can be changed for each occasion...orange, black and white at Halloween, red and green at Christmas. Stand the skewers in a vase for a fun edible table decoration, or place them in cellophane bags for party favors.

assorted colored candy sprinkles
1/2 c. semi-sweet chocolate
   chips or colored chocolate
   melting discs
2 doz. bakery doughnut holes
assorted small tubes piping gel
4 to 6 wooden skewers

Place sprinkles in several small dishes; set aside. In a microwave-safe dish, microwave chocolate on high 30 seconds at a time, until melted. Stir until smooth. Let cool slightly; pour into a plastic zipping bag and snip off a tiny corner. Squeeze chocolate onto doughnut holes, piping designs or funny faces. With a small pastry brush, spread piping gel in stripes, dots or as desired. Roll in sprinkles. Allow to dry for about 10 minutes. Slide 5 to 6 doughnut holes onto each skewer. Makes 2 dozen.

A muffin tin makes a handy container when you're decorating with lots of different sprinkles and colored sugars.

Homemade Caramel Corn

Sophia Graves
Okeechobee, FL

A lady I work with made this recipe for a fundraiser and when I tasted it, this brought back such memories of Halloween past. Fall carnivals always used to sell caramel corn...it was a treat we only received once a year. Once you start eating, it is really hard to stop!

16 c. popped corn
1-1/2 c. salted peanuts
1-1/2 c. sugar
3/4 c. butter, sliced

1/2 c. dark corn syrup
1 t. vanilla extract
1/2 t. baking soda

Place popcorn in a roaster pan; discard any unpopped kernels. Sprinkle peanuts evenly over the top; set aside. In a heavy saucepan over medium heat, combine sugar, butter, corn syrup and vanilla. Bring to a boil while stirring. Reduce heat until simmering. Continue cooking and stirring until a caramel color appears. Remove from heat; stir in baking soda. Pour sugar mixture over popcorn mixture; stir with a large spoon until coated. Bake, uncovered, at 250 degrees for one hour, stirring every 15 minutes. Cool before serving. Store in a covered container. Makes 18 cups.

Hot Mulled Cider

Kathy Grashoff
Fort Wayne, IN

When the evening is crisp and you've come home from a football game or an evening walk, warm up with this delicious cider!

1 gal. apple cider
1 c. light brown sugar, packed
9 whole cloves

9 whole allspice berries
4 3-inch cinnamon sticks
Optional: 2 to 3 lemons, sliced

In a large stockpot, combine cider and brown sugar over medium-high heat. Tie up spices in a cheesecloth square; add to pot. Simmer 5 to 10 minutes; stir until sugar dissolves. Pour cider into mugs. Add a slice of lemon to each mug, if desired. Makes 12 to 16 servings.

Pumpkin Bars with Cream Cheese Icing

Kay Turner
Slocumb, AL

*This recipe has been a favorite in my family for 40 years!
My children used to request it for their birthday cake. I decorate it
for the season, adding a little orange coloring to the icing.*

2 c. sugar
1 c. oil
4 eggs, beaten
2 c. canned pumpkin

2 c. all-purpose flour
2 t. baking powder
1 t. baking soda
1 t. cinnamon

In a large bowl, mix together sugar, oil, eggs and pumpkin; mix well.
Add remaining ingredients; stir well. Pour batter into a greased
15"x10" jelly-roll pan. Bake at 350 degrees about 45 minutes, until
a toothpick tests done when inserted in the center. Cool; spread with
Cream Cheese Icing. Cut into bars. Makes 1-1/2 to 2 dozen.

Cream Cheese Icing:

8-oz. pkg. cream cheese,
   softened
1/2 c. butter

2 t. vanilla extract
3 c. powdered sugar

In a bowl, blend together cream cheese, butter and vanilla. Gradually
stir in enough powdered sugar to make a thick icing.

Halloween party poppers! Fill cardboard tubes with candy
and small treats, then wrap each tube in tissue paper,
securing the ends with curling ribbon. Dress up
the tissue paper with spooky stickers.

Caramel Apples

*Ginny Watson
Scranton, PA*

Caramel apples are the stuff of fall festivals and Halloween carnivals! With each messy bite, they bring out the child in us all.

6 Granny Smith apples
6 wooden craft sticks
14-oz. pkg. caramels,
　unwrapped
1 T. vanilla extract

1 T. water
2 c. chopped pecans or peanuts,
　toasted
Optional: 12-oz. bag semi-sweet
　chocolate chips, pecan halves

Wash and dry apples; remove stems. Insert a craft stick into stem end of each apple; set aside. Combine caramels, vanilla and water in a microwave-safe bowl. Microwave on high 90 seconds or until melted, stirring twice. Dip each apple into the caramel mixture quickly, allowing excess caramel to drip off. Roll in chopped nuts; place apples on lightly greased wax paper. Chill at least 15 minutes. If desired, to make chocolate-dipped caramel apples, microwave chocolate chips on high 90 seconds or until melted, stirring twice; cool 5 minutes. Pour chocolate where craft sticks and apples meet, allowing chocolate to drip down sides of caramel apples. Press pecan halves onto chocolate, if desired. Chill 15 minutes or until set. Makes 6 apples.

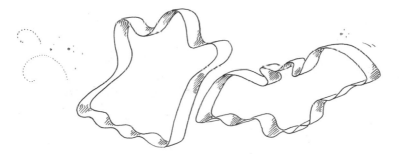

To create frosting in extra-bright seasonal colors, check a craft or cake decorating supply store for paste-style food coloring. Just a little goes a long way!

Chocolate Chip Pudding Cookies

Kathy Vatthauer
Red Lake Falls, MN

For more than 30 years, I've always had an ice cream pail full of these yummy cookies on hand to share at our many school, church, sports and 4-H events. They also freeze very well.

1 c. butter, softened
3/4 c. brown sugar, packed
1/2 c. sugar
3.4-oz. pkg. instant vanilla
    pudding mix

2 eggs, beaten
1 t. vanilla extract
2-1/4 c. all-purpose flour
1 t. baking soda
6-oz. pkg. milk chocolate chips

In a large bowl, combine butter, sugars and dry pudding mix; stir together. Add eggs and vanilla; stir until mixed. Add flour, baking soda and chocolate chips; stir until mixed. Drop teaspoonfuls of dough onto greased baking sheets. Bake at 350 degrees for 10 to 12 minutes, until lightly golden. Makes 2 dozen.

Betty's Picnic Cake

Diane Holland
Galena, IL

I lost my dear sister-in-law to cancer this year. I was always telling her to send you this recipe, so now I am doing it in her memory. It's a great cake for picnics, since it doesn't need any frosting.

3.4-oz. pkg. cook & serve
    chocolate pudding mix
2 c. milk
18-1/2 oz. pkg. chocolate
    cake mix

1/2 c. semi-sweet chocolate
    chips
1/2 c. chopped pecans

Cook dry pudding mix with milk as package directs. Remove from heat; add dry cake mix to hot pudding and stir well. Pour batter into a greased 13"x9" baking pan. Sprinkle with chocolate chips and nuts. Bake at 350 degrees for 25 to 30 minutes. Makes 12 servings.

Frosted Banana Bars

Dana Rowan
Spokane, WA

I have been making this recipe for years. It is always requested when we have a work potluck and there are never any leftovers... ever! I have a friend who is an extremely picky eater. This is one of the only desserts she will eat. She started calling it "Frosted Sin" because it is so yummy and decadent. It is easy to make and a great way to use up extra bananas that are sitting around your kitchen.

1/2 c. butter, softened	2 c. all-purpose flour
2 c. sugar	1 t. baking soda
3 eggs, beaten	1/8 t. salt
1-1/2 c. ripe bananas, mashed	Optional: chopped nuts, sliced
1 t. vanilla extract	bananas

In a large bowl, blend butter and sugar until light and fluffy. Beat in eggs, bananas and vanilla. In a separate bowl, combine flour, baking soda and salt; stir into butter mixture, just until blended. Spread batter in a greased 15"x10" jelly-roll pan. Bake at 350 degrees for 20 to 25 minutes, until a toothpick inserted in the center tests clean. Allow to cool completely; spread with Powdered Sugar Frosting. Garnish with nuts and sliced bananas, if desired. Cut into bars. Makes 3 dozen.

Powdered Sugar Frosting:

8-oz. pkg. cream cheese, softened	4 c. powdered sugar
1/2 c. butter, softened	2 t. vanilla extract

In a large bowl, beat cream cheese and butter until fluffy. Add powdered sugar and vanilla; beat until smooth.

Toting along a frosted dessert? Make sure the frosting will still look party-perfect when you arrive. Insert toothpicks halfway into the dessert before covering in plastic wrap... they'll keep the plastic wrap from touching the frosting.

Cranberry Bread Pudding

Sandra Sullivan
Aurora, CO

This is the ultimate comfort food. It's a favorite fall recipe for when time is short and the oven is full. You can substitute half-and-half for the whole milk or add chopped dried apples or other dried fruits for a tasty twist.

4 c. whole milk
4 eggs
1 c. sugar
2 t. vanilla extract
1/2 t. salt
Optional: 2 T. brandy

6 c. white bread cubes, toasted
1-1/2 c. sweetened dried
   cranberries
Garnish: powdered sugar,
   whipped topping

In a bowl, beat milk, eggs, sugar, vanilla, salt and brandy, if using. Place bread cubes and cranberries in a large slow cooker; drizzle egg mixture over bread mixture. Stir to coat evenly. Cover and cook on low setting for about 3-1/2 hours, just until pudding is set. Sprinkle servings with powdered sugar and top with a dollop of whipped topping. Makes 8 servings.

Stock up on fresh cranberries when they're available every autumn to add their fruity tang to cookies, quick breads and sauces year 'round. Simply pop unopened bags in the freezer.

Pistachio Moon Melts

Linda Belon
Wintersville, OH

These tender tea cookies will melt in your mouth.

1 c. butter, softened
1/3 c. sugar
1-1/2 c. all-purpose flour
1/4 c. cornstarch
1 T. lemon zest

1 t. vanilla extract
1 c. pistachio nuts, toasted
   and finely chopped
1 c. powdered sugar

In a large bowl, combine butter and sugar; beat with an electric mixer on medium speed until creamy. Reduce speed to low; add remaining ingredients except pistachios and powdered sugar. Beat until well mixed. Stir in pistachios. Form dough into 3/4-inch balls; shape balls into crescent shapes. Place one inch apart on ungreased baking sheets. Bake at 325 degrees for 11 to 14 minutes, until set and golden. Let stand 5 minutes; remove cookies from baking sheet. Roll cookies in powdered sugar while still warm; roll in sugar again when cool. Makes 4 dozen.

Pick up a handful of fabric "fat quarters" in fun fall prints at the fabric store to turn into table napkins. Fat quarters measure 22 by 18 inches, so you just need to trim them to 18 inches square, hem the edges and stitch on rick rack in contrasting colors. Scraps are perfect for jar toppers or other small crafts.

Autumn Apple Cookies

Kelly Patrick
Ashburn, VA

Over 15 years ago, my Aunt Shirley first made these delicious cookies for our annual Thanksgiving Day dinner. I got this recipe from her then and I've been making them ever since, as soon as the weather turns cooler and I can bake with the windows wide open. The aroma is amazing, and the flavor is even better!

1 c. raisins
1 c. boiling water
1-1/2 c. shortening
1-1/3 c. light brown sugar, packed
1 egg, beaten
2 c. all-purpose flour
1 t. baking soda

1/2 t. salt
1/2 c. milk
1 c. Golden Delicious apples, peeled, cored and finely chopped
1 c. chopped walnuts, toasted if desired

Combine raisins and boiling water in a bowl; let stand for 10 minutes and drain. Meanwhile, in a bowl, blend shortening, brown sugar and egg; set aside. In a separate large bowl, combine flour, baking soda and salt. Add half of flour mixture to shortening mixture; stir well. Stir in remaining flour mixture and milk. Fold in remaining ingredients. Drop dough by teaspoonfuls onto ungreased baking sheets. Bake at 400 degrees for 9 to 10 minutes, checking after 8 minutes. Cool cookies on baking sheets for 5 minutes; remove to a wire rack and cool. Drizzle with Vanilla Glaze while cookies are still a little warm. Makes 3 dozen.

Vanilla Glaze:

1-1/2 c. powdered sugar
1 t. butter, melted
1/4 t. vanilla extract

1/8 t. salt
2-1/2 t. milk

Mix together all ingredients until smooth.

Keep fresh-baked cookies soft and delicious. Simply tuck a slice of bread into the cookie jar or storage bag.

Mother-Daughter Oatmeal-Raisin Cookies

Sherry Sheehan
Phoenix, AZ

My mom always made the best oatmeal-raisin cookies. I think she used the recipe from the back of the oatmeal box. When going through her cookbook from the early 1950s, I found her vintage recipe. I made a few changes using updated ingredients and methods. They still taste like the ones she made when I was a child! I think she would have been pleased with my changes.

1 c. butter-flavored shortening
1 c. light brown sugar, packed
1 c. sugar
2 eggs, beaten
1 t. vanilla extract
1-1/2 c. all-purpose flour
1 t. baking soda
1 t. salt
1/2 t. cinnamon
3 c. old-fashioned oats, uncooked
Optional: 1/2 c. raisins, 1/2 c. chopped walnuts

In a large bowl, blend shortening and sugars. Add eggs and vanilla; beat well. Add flour, baking soda, salt and cinnamon; mix well. Stir in oats; add raisins and/or nuts, if desired. With a cookie scoop, add dough to parchment paper-lined baking sheets, using 2 tablespoons dough per cookie. Bake at 350 degrees for 12 to 15 minutes, until golden. Let cool for several minutes; remove cookies to a wire rack to finish cooling. Makes 3 dozen.

Découpage a copy of Grandma's favorite cookie recipe onto the lid of a tin...such a sweet keepsake!

Grandma Lind's Fudge

Adonna Mullen
Panama City, FL

This recipe was my grandmother's favorite. I remember staying with her when I was a little girl and I would get so excited to help Granny make her fudge. Granny always eyeballed everything and used a pinch of this & that. She has been gone for 15 years now. When I think of her, I always make a pan of her delicious fudge.

1 c. creamy peanut butter
1/2 c. butter
3/4 c. milk
2-1/2 c. sugar
1/2 c. baking cocoa

1 T. corn syrup
1/8 t. salt
1 t. vanilla extract
Optional: 1 c. chopped walnuts

Prepare a lightly buttered 9"x9" baking pan; set aside. Place peanut butter and butter on a saucer; set aside. In a large heavy saucepan over medium-high heat, combine milk, sugar, cocoa, corn syrup and salt. Cook, stirring constantly, until mixture starts to boil and reaches the soft-ball stage, or 234 to 243 degrees on a candy thermometer. Remove from heat; stir in vanilla, peanut butter, butter and walnuts, if using. Beat by hand until mixture thickens; pour into pan. Let stand until set; cut into small squares. Makes about 3 dozen.

Peanut Butter Fudge:

Simply omit baking cocoa from above recipe.

Mmm...super-size fudge cups! Just spoon warm fudge into foil muffin cups. Wrap individually in squares of colorful cellophane.

Apple Pie Fudge

Audra Vanhorn-Sorey
Columbia, NC

This fudge is a little different...such a wonderful fall treat!

3 c. white chocolate chips
12 gingersnaps, finely crushed
1/2 c. apple pie filling
3 c. sugar
3/4 c. butter

1 c. whipping cream
1/8 t. salt
1 t. cinnamon
1/2 t. nutmeg
1/2 t. allspice

Line a 8"x8" baking pan with parchment paper, leaving "handles" at each side; set aside. Combine chocolate chips, cookie crumbs and pie filling in a bowl. Beat with an electric mixer on low speed; set aside. In a large saucepan over medium heat, combine remaining ingredients. Bring to a rolling boil; cook, stirring constantly, for 4 minutes. Remove from heat. Quickly pour over chocolate chip mixture. Beat on medium speed until chocolate melts, about 2 minutes. Pour into pan. Refrigerate for 3 hours, until set. Lift fudge by paper handles to a cutting board. Cut into small squares. Makes 2 dozen.

Fruit & Nut Bark

Lisa Hains
Ontario, Canada

This unusual recipe is a special favorite that I created. It is pretty on a dessert tray...makes a wonderful quick gift.

24-oz. pkg. white melting
  chocolate
1/2 c. crispy rice cereal
1/2 t. cinnamon
2/3 c. flaked coconut

1 c. peanuts, or chopped walnuts
  or almonds
1/3 c. dried fruit, dried
  cranberries, raisins
  or dates

Melt chocolate according to package instructions; stir in cereal and cinnamon. Stir in remaining ingredients. Pour onto a lightly greased rimmed baking sheet; smooth to edges with the back of a spoon. Chill; break into pieces. Refrigerate or freeze in a plastic zipping bag. Makes 2 to 3 dozen.

Apple Custard Tart

Jennie Gist
Gooseberry Patch

Looking for something different in apple pie? This tart looks impressive and tastes scrumptious, but it's not hard to make. If you don't have a tart pan, just use a 9" pie plate.

9-inch pie crust, unbaked
14-oz. can sweetened condensed
   milk
1-1/2 c. sour cream
1/4 c. frozen apple juice
   concentrate, thawed
1 egg, beaten

1-1/2 t. vanilla extract
1/4 t. cinnamon
1 T. butter
2 Granny Smith or Gala apples,
   peeled, cored and thinly
   sliced

Arrange pie crust in an 11" tart pan. Bake at 375 degrees for 15 minutes, or until lightly golden; cool. Meanwhile, combine remaining ingredients except butter and apples in a bowl. Beat with an electric mixer on medium speed until smooth. Pour into cooled pie crust. Bake at 375 degrees for 25 minutes, or until set in the center. Cool in pan for one hour on a wire rack. In a large skillet, melt butter over medium heat. Sauté apples until tender. Arrange apple slices on top of pie; drizzle with Cinnamon Glaze. Cover and chill at least 4 hours before slicing. Serves 8 to 10.

Cinnamon Glaze:

1/4 c. frozen apple juice
   concentrate, thawed

1 t. cornstarch
1/4 t. cinnamon

Combine ingredients in a small saucepan. Cook and stir over low heat until thickened.

Pick up a new-to-you fall fruit like quince, persimmon or pomegranate at a farmstand. Ask the vendor how to prepare them...he or she is sure to have some tasty suggestions to share!

Traditional Pumpkin Pie

Leona Krivda
Belle Vernon, PA

Soon as fall comes, everyone wants me to make my pumpkin pies. My husband Alan and granddaughter Courtney both want one instead of cake for their fall birthdays. My grandson Jensen always wants one for his Halloween party. I always have to make extras!

2 9-inch pie crusts, unbaked	1 t. salt
4 eggs	2 t. cinnamon
3 c. canned pumpkin	1 t. ground ginger
3-1/3 c. evaporated milk	1/2 t. ground cloves
1-1/2 c. sugar	Garnish: whipped cream

Arrange each pie crust in a 9" pie plate; pinch the edges. Pierce the bottom and sides of crusts with a fork and set aside. In a large bowl, combine remaining ingredients except garnish. Whisk well and divide evenly between the 2 crusts. Bake at 425 degrees for 15 minutes. Turn oven down to 350 degrees; bake for an additional 45 minutes. If crust rims are browning too quickly while baking, cover with strips of aluminum foil. Let cool before cutting. Garnish individual slices with whipped cream. Makes 2 pies, 8 servings each.

Beautify your pie! Roll out extra pie crust, cut out tiny fall leaves with cookie cutters and place them all along the rim of the pie plate before baking.

MawMaw's Pecan Pie

Amanda Ellerbe
Santa Anna, TX

This is the pie my grandmother always made at Thanksgiving and Christmas. It was everyone's favorite...still is!

3 eggs, beaten
2/3 c. sugar
2/3 c. light corn syrup
1 t. vanilla extract

2 c. pecan halves or chopped
   pecans
9-inch pie crust, unbaked

Combine eggs, sugar and corn syrup in a bowl; stir thoroughly. Stir in vanilla and pecans. Pour into unbaked pie crust. Bake at 350 degrees for 45 minutes, or until a toothpick inserted into center tests clean. Set pie on a wire rack; cool completely before slicing. Makes 8 servings.

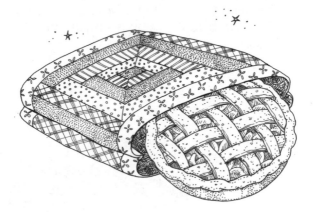

Taking a fresh-baked cobbler or pie to a family get-together? Keep it warm in a cobbler cozy...simple to make! Lay 2 placemats together, wrong-side out. Stitch 3 sides together, leaving one of the short ends open. Turn right-side out...ready to tuck in your dessert!

Fluffy Pumpkin Tartlets

Andrea Heyart
Savannah, TX

Perfect for a mini dessert, a sweet appetizer or a buffet item! Any leftover pumpkin mixture can be spread on bagel or toast, or added to your evening coffee for a yummy pumpkin spice latte.

2 8-oz. tubes refrigerated
   crescent rolls
2 c. whipping cream
1/3 c. sugar
2 t. vanilla extract

15-oz. can pumpkin
8-oz. jar marshmallow creme
1/2 t. pumpkin pie spice
Optional: additional pumpkin
   pie spice

Separate the rolls in one tube into 2 halves; press seams together. Cut each half into 12 equal squares. Press each square into an ungreased mini muffin cup. Repeat with remaining tube of rolls. Bake at 350 degrees for 9 to 11 minutes, until puffed and golden. Let cool for 2 to 3 minutes; remove tartlet crusts to a wire cooling rack. In a bowl, beat cream, sugar and vanilla with an electric mixer on medium-low speed for several minutes, until thick and fluffy. Set aside. In a separate bowl, mix together pumpkin, marshmallow creme and spice until well blended. Fold in 2 cups of whipped cream mixture; stir until no white streaks remain. At serving time, spoon 2 teaspoons of pumpkin mixture into each tartlet crust. Garnish with remaining whipped cream and additional spice, as desired. Makes 2 dozen.

A grandmother pretends she doesn't know who
you are on Halloween.

-Erma Bombeck

Easy Cherry Cobbler

Melonie Klosterho
Fairbanks, AK

This is a fun treat to celebrate Presidents' day in February.
Our entire family loves this dessert!

15-oz. can tart red cherries
1 c. all-purpose flour
1 c. sugar, divided
1 c. 2% milk
2 t. baking powder

1/8 t. salt
1/4 c. butter, melted
Optional: vanilla ice cream or
   whipped topping

Bring cherries with juice to a boil in a saucepan over medium heat; remove from heat. Mix flour, 3/4 cup sugar, milk, baking powder and salt in a medium bowl. Pour butter into 6 one-cup ramekins or into a 2-quart casserole dish; pour flour mixture over butter. Add cherries; do not stir. Sprinkle remaining sugar over top. Bake at 400 degrees for 20 to 30 minutes. Serve warm with ice cream or whipped cream, if desired. Serves 8.

I come from a family with five siblings and my parents. My mom's kitchen was the smallest room in our home. But the best memory was the smell of the kitchen in the fall. We always had homemade bread and apple pie with our evening meals! When we all came home from school and work I don't think we could have felt more loved when we walked into Mom's kitchen and smelled the bread and pie baking and saw Mom's sweet smile to greet us, this was just the best. I'll never forget it. Thanks, Mom.

-RuthAnn Houle, Massena, NY

Nada's Pumpkin Roll

Shirley Verna
Philadelphia, PA

I received this recipe from my dear friend Nada. When we had our quilting class at our church, we all ate lunch together and we took turns bringing a dessert. In the fall and at Christmastime she would always make us this special dessert. We loved it!

3 eggs, beaten	1 t. baking soda
1 c. sugar	1 t. cinnamon
2/3 c. canned pumpkin	Garnish: powdered sugar
3/4 c. all-purpose flour	

In a bowl, beat together eggs and sugar; add remaining ingredients except garnish. Pour batter into a greased and floured 15"x10" jelly-roll pan. Bake at 375 degrees for about 15 minutes, or until cake tests done with a toothpick; don't overbake. Cool; spread cake with Cream Cheese Filling. Carefully roll in waxed paper; refrigerate for 2 hours. To serve, cut into slices; sprinkle with powdered sugar. May be frozen. Makes 8 servings.

Cream Cheese Filling:

8-oz. pkg. cream cheese, softened	1 c. powdered sugar
1/4 c. butter	1/2 t. vanilla extract

In a large bowl, beat cream cheese and butter until fluffy. Beat in powdered sugar and vanilla until smooth.

Try s'mores cones for a tasty new treat! Fill waffle cones with mini marshmallows and chocolate chips. Wrap well in aluminum foil and place at the side of a campfire for a few minutes. Unwrap and enjoy...ooey-gooey!

Frozen Peach Cheesecake

Lisa Smith
Alberta, Canada

I enjoy this flavorful cheesecake. It makes a great cool addition to a holiday dessert table.

1/3 c. butter, melted
1/4 c. graham cracker crumbs
1/4 c. sugar
2 8-oz. pkgs. cream cheese, softened
14-oz. can sweetened condensed milk

2 T. lemon juice
1 to 2 t. almond extract
29-oz. can peach halves, drained
2 c. whipping cream, whipped

In a bowl, mix together butter, graham cracker crumbs and sugar. Press into the bottom of a 13"x9" baking pan; set aside. In a separate bowl, beat cream cheese with an electric mixer on medium speed until fluffy. Beat in condensed milk; stir in lemon juice and extract. Process peaches in a blender until smooth; stir into cream cheese mixture. Fold in whipped cream; spoon mixture over crust layer in pan. Cover and freeze for several hours to overnight before serving. Cut into squares. Makes 12 servings.

Dollop fresh whipped cream on homemade desserts...irresistible!
Pour a pint of whipping cream into a deep, narrow bowl. Beat with
an electric mixer on medium speed, gradually increasing
to high speed. When soft peaks form, add sugar to taste.

Strawberry Glaze Frozen Dessert

*JoAnn
Gooseberry Patch*

*A fresh and fruity dessert to make ahead. At serving time,
just pull from the freezer...so handy!*

2-1/4 c. graham cracker crumbs
3/4 c. butter, melted
1-1/2 c. sugar, divided
1/2 gal. vanilla ice cream,
    softened

1/2 c. pineapple juice
1/4 c. cornstarch
2 c. frozen strawberries, thawed

In a bowl, mix together graham cracker crumbs, butter and 1/2 cup sugar. Press into the bottom of a 13"x9" baking pan. Bake at 225 degrees for 15 minutes; remove from oven and cool completely. Spread ice cream over baked crust; place in freezer. In a saucepan over medium heat, cook pineapple juice, cornstarch and remaining sugar until thick, stirring constantly. Mix in strawberries and let cool. Spread over ice cream; cover and return to freezer until serving time. Cut into squares. Makes 12 servings.

Slice frozen desserts in a jiffy! Let stand at room temperature
for a few minutes, then slice with a thin, sharp knife,
dipped often in hot water.

Maple-Carrot Cupcakes *Lisa Ann Panzino DiNunzio*
Vineland, NJ

This recipe is a favorite among family, friends and our church folks!
My grandmom, now in her 90s, made this recipe as a cake for many,
many, many years. Now I'm making cupcakes. Yummy!

2 c. all-purpose flour
1 c. sugar
1 t. baking powder
1 t. baking soda
1 t. cinnamon
1/2 t. salt

4 eggs, beaten
1 c. safflower oil
1/2 c. maple syrup
3 c. carrots, peeled and grated
Optional: chopped walnuts

In a large bowl, combine flour, sugar, baking powder, baking soda, cinnamon and salt; mix well. In another bowl, beat eggs, oil and syrup. Stir egg mixture into flour mixture, just until moistened. Fold in carrots. Fill greased or paper-lined muffin cups 2/3 full. Bake at 350 degrees for 20 to 25 minutes, until a toothpick inserted in the center tests clean. Cool in pan for 5 minutes; remove cupcakes to wire racks. Spread cooled cupcakes with Maple Frosting; sprinkle with walnuts, if desired. Keep refrigerated. Makes 1-1/2 dozen.

Maple Frosting:

8-oz. pkg. cream cheese,
   softened
1/4 c. butter, softened

1/4 c. maple syrup
1 t. vanilla extract

Combine all ingredients in a bowl; beat until smooth.

Make the sweetest "acorns" in a jiffy! With a dab of frosting,
attach a mini vanilla wafer to a milk chocolate drop.
Add a "stem" made from a bit of pretzel.

Zucchini-Spice Cupcakes

Robyn Martin
Minot, ND

I've been making these cupcakes for years...they are one of my family's absolute favorites! The caramel frosting is simply wonderful.

3 eggs, beaten
1-1/3 c. sugar
1/2 c. oil
1/2 c. orange juice
1 t. almond extract
2-1/2 c. all-purpose flour

2 t. baking soda
1 t. salt
2 t. cinnamon
1/2 t. ground cloves
1-1/2 c. zucchini, shredded

In a large bowl, beat eggs, sugar, oil, orange juice and extract. In a separate bowl, mix remaining ingredients except zucchini; add to egg mixture and mix well. Add zucchini and mix well. Add aluminum foil liners to muffin cups. Fill muffin cups 2/3 full. Bake at 350 degrees for 20 to 25 minutes. Cool cupcakes in pan for 10 minutes before removing to a wire rack. Spread cooled cupcakes with Caramel Frosting. Makes 1-1/2 dozen.

Caramel Frosting:

1 c. brown sugar, packed
1/2 c. butter, sliced
1/4 c. milk

1 t. vanilla extract
1-1/2 to 2 c. powdered sugar

Combine brown sugar, butter and milk in a saucepan; bring to a boil over medium heat. Cook and stir for 2 minutes. Remove from heat; stir in vanilla. Cool to lukewarm. Gradually beat in powdered sugar to a spreadable consistency.

A tasty treat for parties...top frosted cupcakes with candy pumpkins and a sprinkle of green-tinted coconut "grass." Kids will love 'em!

INDEX

INDEX

INDEX

Find Gooseberry Patch
wherever you are!

www.gooseberrypatch.com

Email Blog You Tube

Call us toll-free at 1·800·854·6673

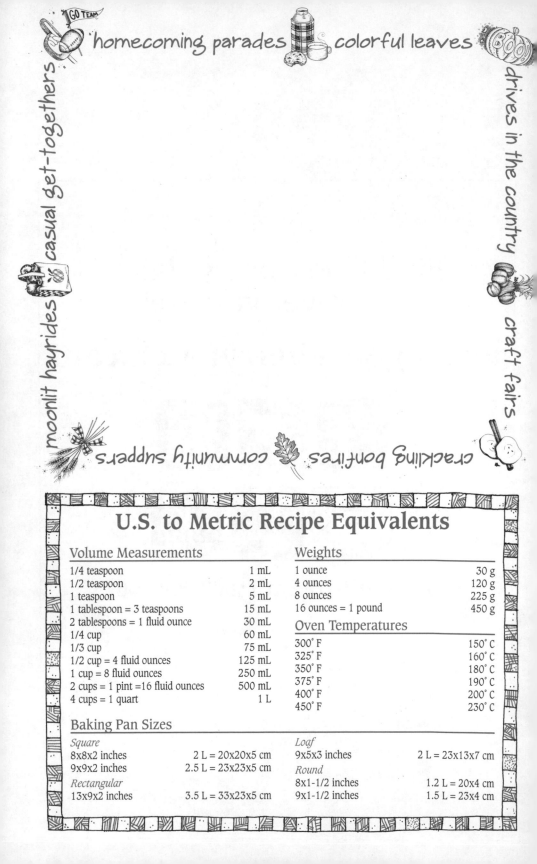

homecoming parades   colorful leaves

casual get-togethers

drives in the country

moonlit hayrides

craft fairs

crackling bonfires   community suppers

U.S. to Metric Recipe Equivalents

Volume Measurements

1/4 teaspoon	1 mL
1/2 teaspoon	2 mL
1 teaspoon	5 mL
1 tablespoon = 3 teaspoons	15 mL
2 tablespoons = 1 fluid ounce	30 mL
1/4 cup	60 mL
1/3 cup	75 mL
1/2 cup = 4 fluid ounces	125 mL
1 cup = 8 fluid ounces	250 mL
2 cups = 1 pint =16 fluid ounces	500 mL
4 cups = 1 quart	1 L

Weights

1 ounce	30 g
4 ounces	120 g
8 ounces	225 g
16 ounces = 1 pound	450 g

Oven Temperatures

300° F	150° C
325° F	160° C
350° F	180° C
375° F	190° C
400° F	200° C
450° F	230° C

Baking Pan Sizes

Square

8x8x2 inches	2 L = 20x20x5 cm
9x9x2 inches	2.5 L = 23x23x5 cm

Rectangular

13x9x2 inches	3.5 L = 33x23x5 cm

Loaf

9x5x3 inches	2 L = 23x13x7 cm

Round

8x1-1/2 inches	1.2 L = 20x4 cm
9x1-1/2 inches	1.5 L = 23x4 cm